Mistletoe Winter

Essays of a Naturalist throughout the Year

Roy Dennis

Saraband

Published by Saraband
Digital World Centre, 1 Lowry Plaza,
The Quays, Salford, M50 3UB

ISBN: 9781913393250

Printed and bound in Great Britain by Clays Ltd, Elcograf S.p.A.

1 2 3 4 5 6 7 8 9 10

For Moira

Contents

Autumn

Introduction

This volume of essays has sprung from the lovely feedback I received from readers of my first essay collection, *Cottongrass Summer*, published in the summer of 2020, at the height of the pandemic. Covid-19 made many of us reassess our lives, explore new ways of living and wonder where we were heading next, both personally and environmentally. For the first time in many decades, there were no, or very few, aircraft overhead and the blue skies were unmarked by vapour trails, with their (unseen) greenhouse gas emissions. It reminded some of us that there are costs to cheap travel and frequent holidays for the wealthy. There was, of course, much grief and loss for many families, to whom Covid-19 did not offer the luxury of choice. To others, though, a remarkable opportunity has been offered, should we choose to take it. Can we – for the sake of the planet – use the car less often, walk more, eat more healthily, find a better balance between our work life and our leisure time? The many avenues closed by lockdown may be more obvious, but it has opened up others, unless – of course – we revert to exactly how we were before Covid-19 and leave the planet on the same uncertain path.

I wanted, in writing these essays about nature, to offer an interesting mix. Some celebrate wildlife, but others illustrate the problems and dilemmas we are posing for nature, and wonder what humankind can do about that. The prognosis for the future of mankind is often bleak, because the human population keeps rising, consumes too much and is led by governments that feed us the myth of perpetual growth. There are, though, welcome signs of change to be seen, and we know how incredibly innovative humankind can be when boxed into a corner. Just imagine, for a moment, what the world could achieve in terms of ecological restoration with the amount that's been spent on Covid-19. The former is more essential – taking the long view – than the latter.

Scotland, and Britain overall, has many pressing ecological problems to solve and it's important to think about them with the benefit of historical knowledge, as well as foresight based on experience. I often think 'busy-ness' is mistaken for brilliance. We need time to reflect and the determination to achieve change in our use of, and respect for, our land and seas.

As Aldo Leopold, the wise American ecologist, wrote in 1948: 'One of the penalties of an ecological education is that one lives alone in a world of wounds. Much of the damage inflicted on land is quite invisible to laymen. An ecologist must either harden his shell and make believe that the consequences of science are none of his business, or he must be the doctor who sees the marks of death in a community that believes itself well and does not want to be told otherwise.' I also firmly agree with another of his statements, made well over half a century ago in an essay in *Round River*, about maintaining the entire ecological fabric of planet Earth: 'If the biota, in the course of eons, has built something we like but do not understand, then who but a fool would discard seemingly useless parts? To keep every cog and wheel is the first precaution of intelligent tinkering.'

Roy Dennis

Winter

Mistletoe

The symbolism of nature can be a personal thing. The call of a particular bird, a familiar scent, the certain shade of a favourite flower or the first flush of a particular green in spring can bring with it a vivid memory or a hope of what the coming year has in store. Each of us will have our own signposts in the natural world, signs of wider optimism when a lot of what we hear about in nature is a worry.

For me, mistletoe was a part of my childhood. I now live too far north to find mistletoe growing in trees near my home. But if I go down in winter to the southern half of England, there waiting for me is the classic scene of my childhood: great clumps of mistletoe growing on the bark of deciduous trees, bare of leaves. Many trees are laden with its heavy globes and they strike an iconic outline in the winter landscape.

Mistletoe is closely associated with ancient pre-Christian times but it is, of course, most important to people these days at Christmas time. It was traditional for me as a boy to collect a few sprays of holly berries in the woods and to climb up into one of the gnarled old apple trees to cut a few sprigs of mistletoe. The holly went on the Christmas pudding, the mistletoe hung over a door. But for me, it is the mistletoe's attractiveness for mistle thrushes – giving the bird its name – that has fixed it as one of my personal markers of the natural cycle. This is the thrush that sings so loudly and lustily from the topmost branches in late winter and early spring, sometimes in strong winds, which has given it the lovely country name of 'stormcock'.

Mistletoe berries are white and sappy inside, and mistle thrushes help spread the plant by wiping that stickiness, along with the seeds, from their bills onto branches, or by depositing the seed in their droppings. These large, noisy thrushes protect their 'own' trees, defending mistletoe clumps from other thrushes, and they are bold and determined in their efforts to protect their food supply.

One winter I was with friends looking for potential osprey nest trees in some big woods near Lac de Neuchâtel in Switzerland. There were some very tall deciduous trees and every one of them held good stocks of mistletoe, each tree guarded by a mistle thrush. I often see this behaviour near my home, too, when the local birds guard the best rowan trees laden with red berries and have a real struggle in October, warding off large flocks of field-fares and redwings, recently arrived on autumn migration from Scandinavia. These thrushes are determined. I remember driving along a local road in early winter and noticing a flock of fifteen or so waxwings flying to a rowan tree and immediately scattering. They had another go, fluttering into the red berries but again were repulsed. This time I could see why: a very large, fluffed-up mistle thrush was perched among its harvest of berries. I hope it kept the waxwings away because a flock of them could have stripped that tree in a morning.

What I like best is to look at winter trees, such as tall willows and poplars, on low ground, especially against the light: the distant balls of mistletoe foliage create a very distinctive outline in the countryside. Until the leaves come out on deciduous trees in the springtime, bunches of mistletoe are the only sign of green vegetation. One spring, I was walking in Romania over open grasslands that held a mix of scattered trees. I noticed a great grey shrike ahead of me and I stopped, sat down and watched it. This is one of my favourite visiting birds in winter in Scotland, and I love to see the grey, black and white markings as they perch on tall vantage points such as isolated trees, electricity wires or deer fences. They have become scarcer over the years, but I always remember them fondly, living the winter months in forest bogs and little valleys, often returning to the same sites winter after winter. There they would hunt small birds and small mammals, for this species is like a little raptor in its habits.

The bird I was watching that day in Romania caught something in the grass and flew several hundred metres, straight to a tall tree containing a large ball of green-leaved mistletoe. It flew back towards where he had previously hunted and, after about ten minutes of watching, I saw it catch something again on the ground and fly directly back to the same tree. That was enough for me to know that there was something of interest up there. Shrikes are well known for stashing excess prey in a larder for a later date, so I was well aware that that was what I might find.

I walked to the base of the tree, a young oak, about forty feet high, growing in open country with lots of side branches. I looked up with my binoculars through the bare branches and thought I could see a nest on the topside of the ball of mistletoe. I'd never seen a great grey shrike's nest before, so, even though I was a long way from my friend's house, I couldn't resist the chance to climb up and have a look. I know I shouldn't have done, at my age, just free climbing without a rope, but it was too good a moment to miss. And, given that I was in Romania to study large carnivores, I reckoned I would always make a meal for some brown bear or wolves if I were to kill myself falling.

The climb was well worth it. When the incubating bird flew off, I peered into the nest and was thrilled to see six beautifully brown-patterned eggs. I quickly climbed back down the tree and walked away, so that the shrike could return to incubate.

My eye was now in and about a kilometre further into my walk, I found another nest on top of a ball of mistletoe in a similar oak tree and, watching from a distance, saw the shrike fly in.

The green bundles of mistletoe, which were quite common in that landscape, allowed the great grey shrikes to start egg-laying and incubation before the deciduous trees came into leaf. That part of Romania was clearly a good breeding area for them.

Later, in France, I heard from a friend that a pioneering pair of breeding ospreys had chosen to build their eyrie on top of a large globe of mistletoe. I would have loved to have seen that, for it would have reminded me of Scotland, where golden eagles in Strathspey and white-tailed eagles in Wester Ross have built their eyries and reared their young on twiggy living growths in Scots pine trees. Fulfilling the same function as mistletoe, they look like a nest from a distance, and offer shelter and security to the nesting birds.

So for those of us, like me, who live in northern Scotland, the mistletoe is a reminder of more southern places, while those who live further south can see the iconic balls in the trees on their daily journeys.

Footprints in the snow

Last evening there was a fall of fresh snow on top of old, and this morning I was sure it would be worth a walk up into the woods to look for mammal tracks. When I pulled back the bedroom curtains at dawn, I saw that the stoat that lives in our roof had already crossed the snowy deck, within five metres of where we had still been sleeping. She'd returned, in her beautiful white ermine coat, in mid-December and remembered from last year the small hole allowing her to scramble up behind the cladding and sleep in the roof space above our dining table.

After breakfast I set off for my local walk. There were red squirrel tracks across the lawn, for they are regular visitors to the bird feeders in the garden. At the bottom of the brae I turned right, up the farm road, and noted the first of many distinctive tracks of brown hares, interspersed with the local traffic of pheasants. The farm tractor had been as far as the junction and then turned back to feed the bull, while last week's ruts from a forestry vehicle were still visible but covered in snow.

After going through the forest gate, my normal route takes me up a short hill beside a small river tributary, which finally makes its way to Findhorn Bay. I followed a fox up this track, its footprints telling me that last night it had been down in the fields and then headed back up into the forest. The snow lay three or four inches deep: it was very frosty and the snow that had fallen last night was soft and powdery, not the best for tracking mammals because the prints are sometimes indistinct. I had no difficulty in identifying the next animal, though: an otter had come over the bank, travelled a short distance along the road and then dropped back down into the burn. I wasn't expecting to find one of those this morning, and only a quarter of a mile from my house.

There's a choice of roads at the top of this slope and I decided to take the one straight ahead, the middle forest road that heads upwards into a mature larch wood. There were more hare tracks, as well as the neat slots of roe deer criss-crossing my route. The local red squirrels had been doing the same, bounding across the track from the woods on one side to the trees on the other. It was already pretty clear that the three most common mammals were roe deer, red squirrels and brown hares.

When my wife, Moira, and I walk this way in normal times, as we often do, we are very lucky to see any of these animals. They, of course, may see us. That's why I have always loved to see virgin snow ahead of me when walking or skiing; it's like opening the pages of a book, each creature telling you: 'I've been here, but where I came from and where am I going is not yours to know.'

Next up was a pine marten, meaning a double-back for me to see where it had come from; I followed the tracks down through the first bit of wood. My hunch was that it may have come from a den box that a forest ranger and I erected in a tree nearly ten years ago, in the hope of providing a safe home for the last of the wildcats in this area. Alas, we built it too late and no cat ever used it. I couldn't find the box during a quick search in the thick bit of the woods, but it would not surprise me if the marten had found it. In those years in which I'd put up trail cameras at these boxes along with dead pheasant bait, it would be martens that found it immediately, and there would often be an image of a badger trying to climb the tree to get at the food.

Climbing back up onto the forest road, I followed the marten's footprints for about a hundred yards, and for the last bit of that stretch they were landing on top of fox tracks. The fox had moved from side to side on the road, clearly not in a hurry, while brown hares and squirrels did the same. When I got to the top of the hill I turned down through the big larches, where three or four red deer had been scraping the snow from the vegetation. I followed their path, for I knew that they would know the best place to scramble over the big ditch on the top side of the lower forest road. It was an easy climb out of the hollow onto my return route, and I was still less than a mile from my home.

By now the sun was shining strongly, so splotches of snow were falling out of the larch trees and creating their own tracks in the snow. On this lower and sunny side of the woods there were new tracks to be seen, very small, in short runs and disappearing under the snow. These were wood mice dashing across the dangerous open space that always left them vulnerable to owl attack. I counted about twenty tracks of mice, interspersed with both red and roe deer, in the next couple of hundred yards before I entered the darker wood.

Here were the prints of a much larger pine marten. I tracked it down the road, before it peeled off into a thicket, the trail almost immediately replaced by that of a fox. And then came a brown hare, emphasising how many animals had been padding through these woods during the previous few hours of darkness.

As I walked, I thought of the history of tracking animals in the snows of this bit of forest. If I had walked here twenty years ago, I would almost certainly have seen the prints of a wildcat or the tracks of a capercaillie; both species are now extinct near my home. Forty years ago I would not have found the tracks of pine marten, for then they were only just starting to spread out from the Western Highlands. Red deer would also have been absent then, before the big new conifer plantations allowed them to colonise this lower ground. Living on such fertile land, they are much larger than those in the mountains, and more fertile, with nearly every hind followed by a calf; and it's a joy now to hear the stags roaring in the autumn.

A wet patch on the side of the track gave rise to a short trail of woodcock tracks and then the hares and squirrels again became more frequent as I reached the junction where I had started. And then I saw new human tracks beside mine: someone else had walked up the hill behind me. I would say it was a man, the size of his boot probably eight, smaller then my size tens. I had a sudden flash of history: what if I had been walking here 5,000 years ago and had found an unknown human following my track? I would have wondered who he was. Which tribe did he come from? Should I be frightened? Should I try to find him, with or without my spear raised? For then, early humans' lives were much closer to the mammals that I had tracked this morning. They would have been more worried by the track of an unknown human than they would have been by the original big fauna in these woods – brown bear, wolf, lynx and aurochs.

Before going home, I cut below the back of our garden to a place where the badgers live, but I couldn't find a badger pad to add to my list. With my binoculars I looked across the river to the badger sett on its sandy bank, but it looked very much as though none had come out last evening, for it was really frosty. I squeezed through the fence and into the field near my house where the snow had been scuffed by brown hares and roe deer, the dark soil of a fresh molehill standing stark in the white field. Beside the fence were the signs of a single rabbit. They used to be so common that the previous owners of our house had needed to rabbit-fence the garden, but disease decimated them in 2009 and they are struggling to return.

My walk this morning, from my home, was just less than two miles, yet I had found evidence of ten mammals and two birds. I felt, turning on the kettle for a cup of tea, that I had been reading an absorbing detective tale, one to which I can return again and again when the snow is right.

A four-minute warning

In the 1950s there was much talk of nuclear war. The awesome terror of hydrogen bombs seemed very real to me and my school pals. We worried about being annihilated. We were told there would be a four-minute warning if the Russians attacked. We were also told we must rush indoors and hide under a table, as if that would really have helped. Many children were haunted by bad dreams.

Any bad dreams now are more closely linked to the day-to-day life of our children. Climate breakdown, the chemical contamination of life on Earth, the loss of our insects, plastic pollution and our over-use of the planet's ecosystem by population growth; and now, after recent events, the threat of global pandemics. News reporting nowadays is never-ending, unlike those naïve days of my youth, and more and more young people are getting alarmed. They want something done now, not wait until tomorrow.

Yesterday morning, I drove home from the Cairngorms and saw three smoke clouds rising from the burning of grouse moors. To me, now, that's like sticking a knife into a wound. In Scotland, we must ban large-scale heather and grassland burning, just as straw burning ceased, and immediately start a massive regeneration of woodland and scrub over all our barren spaces. Turning a 'wet desert', as Fraser Darling said back in that nuclear era, into a thriving land to capture carbon, influence weather and water and restore damaged ecosystems. Rewilding on a massive scale should be our long-delayed contribution to planet renewal. It should become anti-social to own and maintain degraded land.

Too few in authority recognise a threat that is greater than the worries of my youth, unless they are purposely burying their heads in the sand. Thank goodness that young people are protesting for the future of our planet – they need to, and they must demand urgent action while there is time. It's important that they do not give up, for they are the future and are unlikely to get much support from many of their elders. I say to them, keep going, and insist on change.

At my age, mild sunny days in February may beat the five-month winters of snow and ice of my youth, but I worry for my family's future. The young need to have hope and they must be in charge of their destinies. Not only do I support lowering the voting age to sixteen years: I would set it even younger. I asked my twelve-year-old daughter, who thought her age was too young to understand the issues, but come on, let's make it fourteen or fifteen. And in these dangerous times, with time running out, I would also remove the vote at sixty years of age: older people have had their chances and in many ways we've failed.

Deep snow, predators and prey

Four days ago, a neighbour of mine, who lives on lower ground a few miles from my home, phoned to say that a barn owl had taken to roosting in her open shed. She hadn't got round to hanging the door, and the bird was making a bit of a mess. I promised to call by the next morning and take a look.

When I walked into the shed, the only sign of the owl were some splashes of white droppings on the garden furniture and a few tiny feathers on a rafter. As we talked, my neighbour decided that the bird could stay until the snow had gone, but I could see that there was plenty of hunting ground nearby, as there was very little snow cover in the open pine forest beside her home.

Up where I live, the snow cover had been about ten centimetres, or four inches, which is generally too deep to allow barn owls to dive through the snow to catch rodents. Last summer I placed a barn owl nest box in an old cattle shed not far from home and on one of my November walks saw that an owl had found it. I'm pleased for its sake, then, to feel a warmer wind from the west today and see the snow gone. That's good news for owls, if less so for voles and mice.

Inland in northern Scotland, many barn owls die if deep snow remains on the ground for several months. This is a consequence of their being the most northerly barn owls breeding in the world, and this at-the-edge-of-range population fluctuates widely. Even in the coldest and most snowy winters, though, some can find prey around the low-lying coastal areas where ivy-curtained coastal caves are their favourite roosts and nest sites. At inland locations, like Strathspey, with colder winter temperatures and higher snowfall, barn owl numbers build up and then crash. Years later, in warmer winters, when lower-ground birds are doing well, the higher altitudes are recolonised.

The depth of snow is important, as it dictates which predators can still get their prey. Red foxes, for example, on the hunt for voles, can plunge through deeper snow than barn owls can. I remember one winter watching, fascinated, as a fox hunted for its next meal in Yellowstone National Park. Through my binoculars, I could see it listening for a rodent underneath the snow, swivelling its ears for precision and then jumping high into the air, so that the weight of its whole body pushed its snout as deep as possible into the snow. In those wintry conditions, it was the only way to get a meal.

The depth of snow, and the length of time it remains, are important factors in the ecology of the northern lands. Here in Scotland, they are becoming extremely variable. I am old enough to remember years when the first snows covered the hill ground in mid-October, when successive falls built up snow cover as deep as a metre, even on level ground, and when no real thaw came to the middle-ground crofts and hill farms until mid-March. In the mountains, of course, it was much later.

It is in these conditions that voles and mice really thrive. The snow arrives when the ground is still relatively warm and it creates a surprisingly effective shield against cold winds and freezing temperatures. The vegetation under the snow is not killed and the ground is not frozen, so rodents capable of living under the deep snow do extremely well. This is noticeable only when the snow melts in the spring, revealing an incredible network of field vole runs and nests. There under the snow – the snow you might have walked or skied over in the winter – lies a whole vole city, safe from most predation until the arrival of the thaw.

Nowadays, our milder winters caused by climate breakdown often bring much less snow. Here in the north, that can cause problems: periods of sharp frosts without snow cover freeze the ground, causing icing in the soil and desiccation of plant material, both made worse by cold, dry winds. These conditions are poor for rodents adapted to living under snow and the big upswings in numbers are less frequent. Spring resurgence is slower when the land is frozen than when an insulating layer of snow melts and seeps into the soil.

The most dramatic impact in my usual haunts is upon the water vole. Unfortunately, most low-ground water voles, which were still in existence in my youth, have been lost. In the Scottish mountains, though, a population, generally black, survives on the higher ground. They are thought to have colonised from Iberia after the Ice Age and are genetically different from the water voles of England. They weigh about 300 grams, ten times the weight of a field vole, so are an important food for the whole range of bird and mammal predators.

In Scotland, a tiny percentage of the original population lives along slow-moving mountain streams on and around the plateaus. They now have to live in a landscape devoid of fringing vegetation, including dwarf willows, which were widespread before the onslaught of sheep, goats and humans, and the recent high densities of red deer.

The one saving grace for the best large population I know is when the snow arrives in October and strong winds blast drifts into all the small river systems. (As an aside, the drifting snow and high winds remove the snow from exposed ridges, to the benefit of mountain hare and ptarmigan.) It's incredible to be out in the fiercest of these storms, which leave snowdrifts in the hollows as hard as cement. Underneath, though, the water voles are doing just fine. Instead of being confined to the sides of the tiny streams, for fear of predation, they are able to spread out under the snow. A snowy winter brings greatly increased home ranges in this under-snow world (the subnivean temperature remains just above freezing), safe from most predators – only weasels can penetrate the tunnel system in search of voles. Keepers who visit the high ground in winter by snow scooter tell me that weasels occur at higher altitudes than the larger stoats.

When I walk these hills and plateaus in May, I always make for the watercourses to marvel at the water vole villages exposed by the melted snow wreaths. Vole pathways may venture up to ten metres from the banks of the streams and there are signs of leftover food stores and deserted dens. Suddenly, with the melting of the snow, life for the water voles returns to the normality of summer: living in a restricted habitat, the lengthening days allowing more scope for predators such as golden eagles, foxes, stoats and wildcats. The one good wildcat population I know is in this special habitat, with water vole no doubt one of the key prey.

The reason for the difference between high-level and low-ground water voles has generally been put down to predation by mink, but I think the six or seven months of security under the snow may be more important. The snowdrifts packed into the small river 'valleys' of the mountain plateaus are surely one of the key reasons for these surviving water vole populations. If, or when, winters become even warmer and snow cover even scarcer, even in our mountains, then the future for water voles is bleak. It could be ameliorated by an accelerated reduction in grazing damage from red deer and sheep, to encourage a widespread recovery of bank-side tall vegetation and woodland scrub, but we need to act quickly. The mountain water voles may be living on a sharper cliff edge than we thought.

*

Note: when writing this, I searched 'life under the snow' and found the results of an interesting scientific experiment in northern Canada. It showed that lemming numbers increased when

snowdrifts, created by installing experimental snow fences, provided more snow cover. A wider search also involved, for me, a
new word – 'hiemal' – which I'd never heard of and so looked up.
It means 'wintry' or 'of winter'. Now I do know it, but I'll never use
it. If only scientists used plain language, the rest of us would learn
a lot more quickly.

Uisge beatha – the water of life

In Scottish Gaelic, *uisge beatha* is a translation of the ancient Latin word for distilled alcohol – *aqua vitae* or 'water of life'. *Uisge* gives us the present-day word 'whisky', but, of course, it's pure water itself that matters. It's thanks to the incredible properties of water – a mix of hydrogen and oxygen – that we are able to have life on this planet at all. I was thinking about this as I walked through the winter woods this morning, looking at the snow plastered on the eastern side of the larches, brought by the mean east wind last night, and then scrunching through the frosty crust of the snow, down onto the track and skidding a bit on an icy surface left by a vehicle. The more you think about water, the more amazing examples of it you can find.

And I don't mean the role it plays in daily existence for most of us – the bits I take for granted every day, like putting on the kettle for tea, having a shower, making the porridge and cleaning my teeth, hardly stopping to think of the nature of water. We cook our food with it, we grow our crops using water, we now make electricity from water, we transport goods and people great distances over the oceans, and nowadays have a myriad of ways in which we can enjoy water and have a close association with it in all its forms. What I'm thinking of here is water's relation to the natural world.

The first simple but important factor is that water runs downhill. If it weren't replenished on the higher ground, there would be no, or very little, 'new' water to keep the rivers, or life, running. There is an incredible variety of different types of water bodies – lakes, ponds, marshes, streams, rivers, estuaries and the open seas – all of them associated with unique habitats, vegetation and animal life. Crucially, the system has to keep running, but who would ever have dreamt up clouds? Who would have come up with the idea that evaporating water, driven by the sun's heat, could rise from the ocean, creating a build-up of clouds which hold water vapour that then blow over the land and precipitate rainfall, especially near mountains? This can result in too much water in some places, in others too little and sometimes none at all in the driest parts of the planet, but without clouds there would be no life on Earth.

And then we come to the cloud-like extras. I'll never forget being in the great coastal forests south of Seattle while sea fog rolled in from the Pacific Ocean, with the branches, twigs and needles of the monster firs and spruces sieving the water droplets from the air, which then ran wet down the trunks, making the whole forest wet – a rain forest. Even on the hill across from my window at home, misty fog, which can hang on that low coastal summit, affects the planted lodge pole pines with problems of dampness and rot – of course, they should never been planted there in the first place. Another water capture technique can also be seen from that same window when I wake up on very cold mornings and look out to find the birches resplendent in hoar frost at sunrise. Sometimes the warming sun melts the frost within a few hours, and the trees drip with water droplets. Once in Strathspey, on a very cold morning, well below −20°C, I was witness to a unique and beautiful event: the tiniest specks of water vapour in the air super-freezing as individual water crystals, which twinkled in the morning sunshine. This recycling of water from the rivers to the sea, back into the clouds as moisture, to return once more to the land as rain, is something very special.

And ice holds a special fascination for me. When the days get shorter in our northern winter, and the air becomes colder, the surface temperature of our freshwater lochs drops, the surface water becomes denser and sinks to the bottom, causing circulation. But at 4°C the water suddenly becomes less dense: it stays at the surface and, at the freezing point, becomes ice. This is a wonderful adaptation, because if lochs froze from the bottom up, most living organisms in the water would be unable to survive. In cold winters the ice becomes thicker and thicker, and I can remember winters when the fresh waters were frozen from late October through to the following spring. In exceptional winters in Scotland, this could result in ice of nearly a foot thick, which allowed the great bonspiels of curling on ice (this required a depth of at least seven inches); sadly, the great gatherings of thousands of curlers on outdoor ice is now a memory. In 1963, in my daft youth, I remember driving my old car onto Loch Garten for fun.

In more northerly countries, of course, the thickly iced lakes become winter highways between villages. One summer, I visited the legendary Lake Baikal in Siberia with a group of UK birdwatchers and, in the little museum on the lake shore, saw photographs of times when the railway track was laid across the ice to offer a major shortcut during the winter months. The ice there can be a metre thick and is beautifully clear.

Frozen lakes are important for wildlife, because the inhabitants' year divides into two parts: life in winter with ice, life in summer without. That's why ospreys leave Scotland for West Africa in the autumn: they cannot stay with us because they would be unable to catch fish during the winter. Fish get a six-month rest from aerial predation until spring melts the ice and brings the migratory species back. Many other forms of wildlife adapt to these changes of living under and over the ice, while frozen lakes also have major impacts on the ranging behaviour of land mammals; instead of being isolated on one side of an extensive lake, they are suddenly able to cross it and meet others of their species on the other shore.

In the true north, wolves, lynxes and foxes find new routes across the ice to islands denied them in summer, or possibly visit and mate with others of their species on the far shore. Herbivores such as moose, deer and hares can also mix with their own kind by travelling over the ice. I guess the important thing is not to be stuck on the wrong side when the ice melts in the spring. But frozen lakes change the nature of the land, even for us humans. In 1980, when we were doing fieldwork for a complete golden eagle survey of the Scottish Highlands the following year, we were very fortunate that the month of February was sunny and very cold. It meant that on long daytime hikes to check distant eyries we could walk with ease across frozen bogs and lochs, which in the summer would have involved much longer journeys. Hiking on frozen land is something special, and cross-country skiing even better.

I've already covered the importance of snow cover for the rodents living below it, and the protection it gives to plant communities (see 'Deep snow, predators and prey'), but snow isn't just snow – there is huge variation in quality and quantity, and with strong winds it can get anywhere. Blown deeply into crevices in rocks and cliffs, it thaws and freezes and helps break up the underlying rocks, which helps with the process of soil creation.

We sometimes wonder what it will take for humanity to protect and cherish our home planet. Given the wonders of Earth's natural processes, we might perhaps just need to reflect a little more when next we get caught in the rain, slip on the ice or see children building a snowman.

Translocating mountain hares

Over millennia, there have been large-scale changes in the original vegetative cover of Scotland, through destruction of natural habitats for agriculture, the encroachment of human living space and, in recent centuries, the drive towards timber production. How has this impacted species like mountain hare?

The species probably benefited from the destruction of the original forests and the creation of open moorland below the montane zone, which was their favoured original habitat. They have declined dramatically in the last and present centuries and are doing so still. Large but declining populations remain in some parts of the eastern Highlands, with culling on grouse moors suggested as a major cause of the fall in numbers, although it sometimes appears that the highest densities still occur on managed grouse moors that carry out culls. Elsewhere there are small, fragmented, much-reduced populations in many areas of the Scottish mountains, and they do not show any signs of increase. It is instructive to read the Victorian record books of distribution and numbers throughout northern Scotland, and ponder why, in many of those locations – Wester Ross, Sutherland, Caithness and Lochaber, for example – they are so scarce, despite the fact that the remaining vegetation is capable of providing sustenance to large numbers of red deer and sheep.

Dispersal in unpressurised natural populations of mountain hares is apparently very local (a few miles or more), so, in consequence, it is likely that fragmented populations may now exhibit inbreeding and loss of genetic variation, possibly severe. It is also possible that when mountain hare numbers fall to very low levels, annual recruitment cannot be sustained in the face of predation by golden eagles and other predators. Historically, in ancient populations, mixing could have been long distance when caused by large-scale natural fires or winters of long-lasting deep snow, and there were no fences in the glens to prevent passage between populations. Many of these populations are now so isolated due to human restraints on the low ground (forestry, agricultural fences, roads and other manmade obstacles) that there is no chance of new individuals arriving naturally and mixing.

It is interesting to speculate on the drivers of population mixing in the distant past in Scotland. Possibly devastating large-scale fires would have pushed hares, living near the boundaries, out into new territories, with consequent mixing of genetic diversity, whilst subsequent natural regeneration of burnt areas would have led to the re-joining of populations from all directions, which could also have improved genetic diversity. Widespread and long-lasting snowy winters were another disperser, forcing hares into the glens where, again, sub-population mixing could take place. Despite the negative impacts of the large hare drives and excessive shooting, this could give genetic mixing benefits to the surviving individuals and their breeding success. On the other hand, inbreeding and declining populations of species living in fragmented areas are recognised in a range of species worldwide.

For some years I have wished to test the efficacy of moving mountain hares from high-density populations, where culling has occurred, to several fragmented populations with very low densities in Sutherland and Lochaber. It seems to me to be a worthwhile alternative to culling and I am sure that some estates will be interested in carrying out positive conservation management. In some ways it would mimic what we have done with red squirrel translocations.

My vision is that this will result in improved breeding in regions with low populations, leading to restored and viable populations.

At present it is tragic to walk for miles through suitable mountain hare habitats on many northern and western mountains without seeing a single hare, and yet know that within a few hundred kilometres, large numbers have been annually culled.

First, I wished to test our ability to live-trap mountain hares outwith the present close season (the non-breeding season) and to carry out translocation efficiently and successfully, with high emphasis on animal welfare. I was sure we could do so and of course took note that the species was subject to many successful translocations in earlier centuries, including non-native introductions to the Western Isles, Orkney and Shetland.

In February 2020 we carried out our first trial translocations to test the best methods of capture and safe handling. The gamekeepers, who allowed us to work with them, were experts in catching mountain hares and in two half-days we moved a total of fifteen hares to Alladale in Sutherland and to Corrour in Lochaber. I am sure this initiative will benefit mountain hare populations overall, in regard to range and numbers. It would restore part of the montane ecosystem and would also benefit species such as golden eagle and wildcat that prey on hares, especially in regions of low prey availability. We have assembled a report of our initial activities – including numbers, sex and biometrics, as well as release sites and techniques – and follow-up monitoring will compare with locational baseline data. I believe this will lead to licence approval for future translocations as an alternative to culling, and hopefully help restore thriving populations of mountain hare to many of their ancient mountain haunts.

Ptarmigan alarm call

I got to know ptarmigan for the first time in the spring of 1960. I had been taken up into the corries of Cairn Gorm to try skiing. The set-up was amazingly basic in those days before the ski road was built, making the mountain accessible to many more people. Somehow, a group of keen skiers had managed to get an old tractor up to the top of the main slope. One back wheel had been jacked up, the tyre removed and a very long manila rope, wound round a couple turns, ran several hundred yards downhill to a big pulley anchored to the ground. One person took turns to keep the tractor running while their friends grabbed the rope and were pulled to the top of the slope for another run. All you had to remember was to let go before hitting the tractor. The skis and gear were also very basic, but it was such fun, especially after work on warm evenings with the low sun shining into the corrie. And, for me, there was the joy of hearing and seeing ptarmigan croaking in the rocks above me, another new bird for a young birder.

That summer I got to know ptarmigan better when I started to explore the mountain plateaus, hiking from Glenmore up Cairn Gorm and then across the superb mountain country to Ben Macdhui or climbing out of Glen Feshie onto the magical slopes of Sgoran Dubh, Braeriach and Cairn Toul. Often in those days I would see no other person, especially if I was birding during the week, and even the ptarmigan were surprisingly unobtrusive. I'd be scrambling up the rocks and suddenly realise I was being watched from twenty paces away by a pair of ptarmigan or a family party, in their buff and grey summer coats. Sometimes they would scuttle away but at other times would burst into flight, revealing their white wings, their croaking calls echoing across the cliffs. In winter, their plumage snow-white, a perfect camouflage for the mountains, they appeared to me as immaculate ghosts.

This was my first experience of getting to know the special hill birds of Scotland on their breeding grounds. Dotterel was the most special. This beautiful, confiding, plover-like wader was new to me during those first summer visits of the early 1960s. One day, I nearly stood on one as it sat on its nest on Cairn Lochan. The bird ran a few feet away from my boot, leaving two eggs, but was eager to get back on. I moved back no more than a few feet and watched it run back on, sit down and, after some shuffling, run off again after laying a third egg. The photograph I took that day was of a female dotterel on its nest. This species has reverse parental duties; normally, when you see a dotterel incubating eggs, it will be the male you are looking at rather than the female.

I had seen snow buntings on migration at Fair Isle the previous year. In that era, it was not unusual to see quite large winter flocks in farm fields and along the coast. Nearly all but a few would migrate to breed in northern countries, while a small number of those beautiful black-and-white buntings nested on the Cairngorm plateaus. They hid their nests in screes and rocks, the male birds singing bravely in the emptiness from a high rock. When the young had hatched, I loved to watch the parents scuttling around the remaining snowfields where they picked up insects, attracted and chilled by the snow, to feed their young. I'm sure long-lasting snowfields are important for this species.

During one of those early winters, I got a job reindeer herding in the Cairngorms to fill in the time between my osprey wardening duties. Mr Utsi, a Lapp from northern Sweden, had established in Glenmore a herd of reindeer, which ranged on the Cairngorms. For several months, I would hike or cross-country ski every day from Reindeer House in Glenmore into the Cairngorms to check the reindeer, count the herd and report my daily findings. I always carried my binoculars and a rucksack containing my gear and food for myself, as well as a couple of packs of Ryvita biscuits. The reindeer just loved them, and rustling the packet was enough to get them to come over and be checked.

My job with the reindeer came to an end when Christmas approached and I was too shy to dress up as Santa Claus and parade through Aviemore. Until that point, though, it had taken me into the territories of some of our hardiest species. I had often been up on the plateau in the snow but spent most of my time in the corries and lower slopes leading down to the forest. On those days, I would come across small flocks of ptarmigan, their calls always enlivening my solitary treks. A passing raven or two would cronk overhead, while snow bunting was the only other regular winter bird capable of living in the freezing temperatures.

And then came the new access road up Cairn Gorm, and access to the high tops became easier. Soon, ski lifts, tows and buildings were installed, while Badenoch and Strathspey became the Spey Valley tourist area for skiing. Hotels in the Highland villages, from Kingussie in the west to Grantown-on-Spey in the east and north to Carrbridge, catered for the booming interest in skiing. It was taken as a given that plenty of snow for skiing would be a never-ending resource for tourism. Big developments were built at Aviemore, with ever-increasing uplift facilities on the mountain culminating in a mountain railway. Passing years saw an ever-increasing demand for skiing, resulting in planning applications to develop more of the mountains, some of which we fought in planning inquiries. It was fortunate that they did not all go ahead, for by the end of the century the changing climate created by man's activities on the Earth were making the arrival of snow, and the length of time it stayed, ever more unpredictable.

In hindsight we should have foreseen all this. We should have understood the impact of humans on the climate, but we just don't seem to be very good at this, even now. I remember as a boy going for a school trip to London on a day of a real 'pea souper' smog. 'Smog' is not a word you come across much now, but hearing it brings back to me the smell and taste of it in my youth, as we stumbled through a noxious mix of fog, soot and gas from coal fires and industry. It was simply accepted that all the big city buildings were covered in soot. It eventually became so bad that a major campaign did reduce coal-burning pollution in the cities, and the buildings were finally cleaned and returned to the colour they had been when they were first built.

In the 1980s, we were still having real winters of snow in Strathspey and it was often deep and crisp. Mountain hares and ptarmigan were in their element in their white winter plumage. One year, a BBC TV director had an idea for a new programme about the restoration of wolves to Scotland and we had several great days filming with three 'tame' wolves in a secure enclosure in the ancient forest, with the branches and forest floor covered in snow. On the second day, the presenter interviewed me as we walked over the hills above the forest through knee-deep snow, with the cameraman filming from a helicopter hovering overhead, blowing the crisp powder snow all around us. It was extremely photogenic in the sun.

The pilot was a old friend of mine and, once the filming was finished, he told me there was a spare hour in the contract and asked if I would like a quick look round the Cairngorms by air, as the conditions and visibility were so perfect. Our route took us direct to Cairn Gorm itself, out over the plateau towards Ben Macdhui and then low above the cliffs overlooking Loch Avon. The recent big snowfall had occurred without winds, so even the ridges were white. Suddenly a great flock of ptarmigan exploded from the snows and hurtled off round the corner of the mountains. There were several hundreds packed together, the biggest flock I'd ever seen, and truly spectacular. They had almost certainly flocked together because they were finding it difficult to get at food in the deep snow and were waiting for the next winds to clear the snow from the exposed ridges, where they could find mountain plants for food.

In the last twenty years, snowfalls have become much more unpredictable. The days have gone when snow started to pack in the mountains in October and was still present in April and May. There are, of course, occasional cold winters and deep snow, as between 2008 and 2010, but where I live in Moray, we hardly see any snow at all in some winters and no longer think to carry shovels, food and sleeping bags in the boot of the car. Life is easier for us but it's certainly becoming more difficult for ptarmigan and mountain hares: it's no good to be snow-white when the land is brown and predators are on your trail. Ptarmigan will likely desert the outlying lower hills first, and it's unlikely that we will ever see very large flocks of them again.

I'm writing this essay during the Covid-19 pandemic, with the heartbreak and damage it has caused across the world at the forefront of my mind. It's clearly another case of our failure to recognise the dangers posed to our way of life by new threats, which can only be worsened by climate breakdown and biodiversity crisis. We need to invest in much better future forecasting, devoting time, money and effort on identifying and solving these environmental and ecological risks and threats, rather than on focussing, as we do at present, on military security and financial globalisation. It's a complex problem illustrated in my mind by a very simple image: a pair of pure white ptarmigan walking on a snow-free mountaintop in winter. We are getting another wake-up call from nature, if we only take the time to listen to it.

Fighting for a special place

I visited Sutherland in February 2019, giving me a chance to look for a pair of sea eagles and to check the spread of the red squirrels we had translocated six years before. My main reason for driving north, though, was to visit the Carnegie Hall.

It's a small place in Clashmore with a very big name – both this Highland village hall and the more famous New York concert venue were built by the philanthropist Andrew Carnegie. I was there to attend the proceedings of the public inquiry into a golf development proposed on the Coul Links Site of Special Scientific Interest (SSSI) near Dornoch. I've known that part of the Sutherland coast since the 1960s for its great birding: big flocks of eiders, with occasional king eiders, eating mussels offshore, and several thousand gorgeous long-tailed ducks spring-displaying in the mouth of the Fleet days before flying to the northern Baltic. The most recent was to watch a couple of rare shore larks scuttling in the wintertime dunes.

I wanted to be there to show support for the people opposed to damaging Coul Links and slipped into a seat at the back of the hall to listen to the proceedings. Hearing the debate brought back memories, from the 1970s onwards, of other inquiries at which my RSPB colleagues and I were questioned by lawyers as we fought to protect one nature site after another. We won some and lost some, and I wonder why we're still having to fight at all.

Our focus in those days was on the protection of birds, and there were many who were unimpressed by that. 'Do you want birds or jobs?' they'd cry. Now, though, things are much more pressing – we desperately need these special areas of nature to ensure the future of our planet.

Outside the hall, it felt like spring rather than the end of February. My car radio told me this was one of the hottest February days on record, in a decade of record-breaking temperatures. I flicked the channel to hear a reporter talking about the massive decline in insects. On another, the Green Party MP was talking about the next day's debate at Westminster on 'climate change' or, better stated, 'climate breakdown'.

As well as being an SSSI, Coul Links (along with neighbouring Loch Fleet National Nature Reserve) is a Ramsar Site and a Special Protection Area. There are just over 1,400 SSSIs in Scotland, covering just under thirteen per cent of our country, so why are we putting any of them at risk now, at a time when we need to protect the environment for the sake of our grandchildren? Some world visionaries believe that to ensure long-term survival of the Earth's ecosystems we will need to have fifty per cent of the planet's land and seas dedicated to nature and natural processes. I am a firm supporter of that target. We simply cannot lose any more nature sites and the huge areas of land degraded by fire and livestock need to be ecologically restored.

Ecological restoration on a large enough scale to attempt to ameliorate the increasing levels of carbon and to restore Earth's ecological processes will be job creation on a truly massive scale. It will require bold, far-seeing political leaders and the diversion of major funding from other budgets. It is no longer a matter of choice. As I listened to the morning's evidence, expert pitted against QC, I also reflected on how antiquated the term 'SSSI' now is. It does not command public respect. In today's perilous times, these places need a rebrand, maybe to something like 'Areas of Ecological Importance'.

After a long wait, the opponents of the golf course did win their case and Coul Links was saved – sadly, as is so often the way, until the next time they have to fight for it. A fresh attempt to reverse the decision has been proposed as I write, in early 2021. Can there be any clearer demonstration that world governments must insist on the essential need to safeguard and restore natural ecosystems, rather than allowing them to be destroyed?

Spring

The uncertain lockdown spring of 2020

It's very strange, in this era of Covid-19, not to be going out bird-ing when the signs of coming spring are beckoning, but at least I have more time these days to watch the goings-on in the garden. The stoat that lives in our roof has turned from white to brown during these first two weeks of our isolation, while Phoebe's nest box, built at Scouts and finally fixed yesterday to the end of her old Wendy house, has attracted a pair of great tits, taking ownership this early morning. As I type, though, I'm thinking of larger birds.

The young white-tailed eagles we released in August 2019 on the Isle of Wight have had a busy few weeks. Despite occasional short wanderings, the four eagles had settled into a winter routine, three staying on the island and one having gone to live with red kites and buzzards in Oxfordshire and Buckinghamshire. Most of their time was spent just sitting in big trees, watching the world go by and learning the life of the countryside, watching in particular other carrion-eaters, for they have been living off dead birds and small mammals, as well as dead deer and a fox. They might also have caught rabbits and a mallard; one may even have hunted grey mullet in an estuary on the Solent. To see four living successfully through their first autumn and winter, and on into April 2020, is a success at the start of the reintroduction project.

Way back in 1968, on Fair Isle, three out of the four young sea eagles that we released there survived the winter on the island before, in spring, the two females departed. In those days we had no idea where they had gone. Those birds were, in fact, never seen again, but I always hoped that, when soaring several thousand feet above that remote Shetland island, they might have seen Norway and headed home. Much later, during the releases of the 1990s in

Wester Ross, one young sea eagle, individually identified by its coloured wing tags, flew north to Shetland and, years later, was proved to be breeding in Norway, so we know that at least one did make the long flight back over the North Sea.

Now, of course, it's all so different. Without leaving my desk I can check each eagle's tiny satellite transmitter on my laptop. Within an hour, the data on each bird's travels will appear on my screen in digital and map form. Despite my being restricted to home I can have a daily catch-up on wild creatures, whose lives continue despite the tragedies affecting the world's human population. Until a month ago, we would generally find each eagle sticking closely to its usual routines, sometimes living for days within a few square kilometres of wooded countryside.

This past month, though, it's started to be very different. My colleagues Tim Mackrill and Steve Egerton-Read are likely to phone me with the latest news before I've got online. One eagle made a big circular flight to Kent and back to the Isle of Wight; the bird wintering in Oxfordshire headed west to the Forest of Dean, north to Stoke and then to Rutland Water. One settled in Wiltshire and later did a day trip to the Somerset Levels and back. Each day brought something new.

And then we got a report of the first immature sea eagle not from the reintroduction, sighted in Wiltshire and Hampshire. It had a metal ring and, with the help of colleagues in Sweden, we established that it was probably from there. Other birds were then reported, from Buckinghamshire to Kent to East Anglia – there was a small influx of mainland European wanderers. We were very grateful to people who sent in photos, as we use them to identify individuals, looking for nicks in their big flight feathers or other distinguishing features.

We always hope that one or more might be attracted to join the Isle of Wight birds, but we also have to accept that these 'new' ones might encourage the island birds to wander. We like to hear of sightings and can invite them without encouraging anyone to leave home base, for these are birds that fly over towns and villages on their journeys. Suburban gardens have already provided us with some great eagle photos.

Eagle behaviour such as this, and that of the bird which returned to Norway, raises a fascinating question: from what distance can one large eagle see another, soaring on a clear day? It looks as if they do go and look for – and maybe follow – each other. I remember how one golden eagle, which I was satellite-tracking in Scotland, flew forty kilometres from Angus to Tentsmuir in Fife to check out a pair of white-tailed eagles, before tracking west to Perthshire. On Saturday, we saw similar behaviour from young sea eagles. One flew from Rutland Water to the south Humber and, yesterday, on to the North York Moors, while another flew from Berkshire to roost overnight just five miles from the Humber bird, then also flying north to the North York Moors. Were they alone? Or were they following a wanderer from over the sea? It's a shame that they are not always observed as they pass overhead, but checking their progress on Google Earth is far more than I could do with those first errant Fair Isle eagles. We are staying home, but they are free to fly, and we can follow them as they go.

Losing our lapwings

I've just had my daily walk from the house. At this time of year, early spring, I always pause at a field gate a mile or so along my road to look for the lapwings. It's a wet field with a couple of springs and it's a grazing field for cattle and sheep. When I first walked this way in the springtime, about eight years ago, there were three pairs of lapwings. It was a joy to watch their daredevil flying and to hear their lovely calls. For my wife and I, these lapwing walks became one of the high points of the starting year.

Last year and the year before that, though, they were down to one and a half pairs. Several times last spring there were, briefly, four in the field, but each time I watched, the fourth would fly off. Was it the wrong sex for the single bird, or did it simply not like what remained of the habitat? Each year, more and more of the grass has been covered by rushes, making the field less attractive to lapwings. This year, there were none. It was with real sadness that we would check the field, noting their absence and gradually giving up hope of seeing them in what we will no doubt, purely out of habit, continue to call 'The Lapwing Field'. We miss the aerobatics and the 'peewit' calls. 'Can't we do something to encourage them back?' asked my wife.

That's very difficult for a species that is used to a style of agriculture I knew when I first moved to Scotland sixty years ago. These fields would then have been in a rotational farming system based principally on dung, lime and careful husbandry, with an output of cereals, turnips, potatoes, cattle and sheep. When I crofted, lapwings loved to nest in the fields sown with spring cereals. The eggs were well hidden and the lapwings could easily see and chase away crows. When I rolled the field, by tractor, I would mark the nests with a couple of stones and the birds would sit tight as I rattled up and down. The markers were then removed and the birds would continue in peace, feeding in fields full of invertebrates.

When they were ready to leave, they would gather in big flocks further south and spend the winters, often alongside golden plovers, feeding on large fields of winter cereals or grazing land. Driving south on the A1, the main road cutting through Yorkshire, I would marvel at these huge, swirling flocks. During the agricultural intensification of the 1970s, these great fields became less and less attractive as the invertebrates declined under chemical farming, and even grasslands proved less appealing as cattle were treated with chemicals and their dung became toxic to the insects on which the birds depended. Meanwhile, the lapwings' summer homes on upland farms and crofts changed dramatically as sheep became the main crop, and traditional mixed agriculture and rotational cropping went into dramatic decline.

I still know just one upland farm in this area where an older farmer keeps up the traditional ways with dunging the fields. It's the one place where I am sure I will still find a few pairs of lapwings breeding, along with a pair of oystercatchers, and usually at least two or three curlews probing the soil for worms, while their mates incubate eggs on the nearby moorland. In early spring, it's also a sure place for small flocks of redwings and fieldfares, feeding up before returning to Scandinavia. The lapwings' future really is that precarious, though: once the old man gives up his traditional ways, they will be gone.

Is it possible to turn things around? I've worked successfully with restoring many species of bird and mammal, but to restore lapwings, or curlews, on a broad scale would be really difficult. It would require a step back to a former age of farming, with no persistent chemicals and an agriculture based on long hours and hard work. I'm not sure that fits with present-day ambitions, but maybe in the future we will need to make a dramatic change in our farming practices, allowing us to live in harmony with the earth and with nature. This morning, though, we can only note and mourn the loss of lapwings from our local life.

Opening gates, opening minds

American poet Robert Frost noted cryptically that good fences make good neighbours, in his poem 'Mending Wall' (1914). What he thought about gates is less clear, but I find them a handy measure of a person's potential.

Every now and then, I'll get an email from a student at university saying they would love to have work like mine. Sometimes I'll invite them for a day or two in the field, looking at ospreys or eagles, often on large private estates where I have permission to use the roads and tracks to monitor nesting pairs. It's great for us to host these young people, talking over supper about fieldwork, hearing about their interests and discussing what the future might look like. Some, though, have noticed that I seem very interested in their ability to open a gate. For me, it's second nature to recognise that a gate over a track opens this way or that – just look at the scuffmarks on the ground or the lie of the hinges. It might seem trivial but opening and closing gates and leaving them as you find them gives owners confidence that you can be trusted. It's an activity that almost immediately reveals the depth of someone's experience in country matters.

I have long believed that an MSc in practical nature conservation and wildlife management, after a first or second degree, is desperately needed. Fieldwork led by biologists, botanists, gamekeepers and foresters is needed by anyone wanting to work successfully with a whole range of land managers. To gain respect from these people, leading to successful partnerships, requires an ability to be confident in any surroundings. A field ecologist working in rewilding must be able not only to identify plants and birds but be able to pick up a feather and know from which species it came, where on the bird's body it belonged and why it might be lying on the forest floor. This overall perspective demonstrates ability and shows respect for a shepherd who can glance at a flock of sheep and see which one is ready to lamb, or a forester who knows the age class of a stand of Scots pine and whether or not the trees are growing well. This hard-won but essential background credibility is your passport to successful and collaborative projects.

Rewilding or ecological restoration, which is essential for the future of the planet, will take place on land presently farmed or forested or on open range. The people on those lands will be very experienced in their own fields, so it is important that ecologists – rewilding specialists – can engage with them on level terms. The field training and mentoring of future rewilding ecologists requires reappraisal, for there is a shortfall in expertise and ability. Excellent young people are coming out of school or university, often with impressive academic achievements, but lacking solid fieldwork experience. This is not surprising: many come from urban backgrounds and the old-style training in field studies is not as prevalent as it once was. Some of that is down to modern health and safety requirements and the burden of responsibility that falls on anyone taking young people into the wilds.

Another area of particular concern for large-scale rewilding is that present-day ecologists are often taught to concentrate on relatively narrow fields. This is very important in some areas of scientific research; you want the person working on vaccines during a pandemic to be a specialist. But restoring the Earth, combatting biodiversity collapse and climate breakdown, does not call for action tomorrow, it calls for it today, and on a very large scale. That can frighten many scientists, who – knowing that they'll be held to account – do not like to be asked for an immediate course of action. A landowner or politician may wish to know how rewilding will have restored an area in, say, fifty years' time. A common response to that question might be: 'Well, we need to do three more years of research, it will cost this much, and then I can tell you.' We no longer have time for that approach. Remember the professors of past generations who carried out their doctorates on entire ecosystems, not on individual organisms? Their broader knowledge and life experiences allowed them to be confident enough to give a straight answer and suggest a course of immediate action as good as any. I think they were also less worried about everything going exactly to plan, for the truth is that there are so many potential stochastic events – chance natural crises such as droughts, floods, storms which destroy entire forests, volcanic ash clouds, avian pandemics and so on – that certainty is impossible. We need people with a breadth of field experience, who are comfortable with science, pragmatic and capable of making concrete recommendations.

A big problem now is the breakdown of frequent contact between conservationists – all too often working from offices – and land managers. In the 1960s, '70s and '80s, the men and women working for the Nature Conservancy were as likely to be out doing fieldwork as they were to be at their desks, particularly in spring and summer. As technological advances have changed our lives, we have reached a point where many, maybe most, conservation staff are desk-bound. An immediate recall of detailed maps and data on the computer screen, the ability to give the appearance of being out in the field when using Google Earth, and advances in the computer modelling of wildlife events, seem to have led to less and less actual fieldwork. The real worry here is a widening gulf between conservationists in their offices and the farmers, foresters, land managers and nature wardens on the ground. It's a gulf that might even result in a kind of fear on the part of senior managers in environmental NGOs or government departments: will a farmer ask them to identify a breed of sheep, a forester point out a rare flower on the forest floor or a landowner pick up a feather or broken eggshell and ask them which species it belongs to? These people's lives are rooted in field knowledge and long experience, and they rate those qualities in a rewilding expert more than the last scientific report that expert read or wrote.

Fieldwork knowledge and experience, gained over many years, is a conservationist's currency. People often tell me I'm lucky to work on exciting projects, but it's not just a question of luck – it's a matter of determination and judging which projects to focus on. In 1990, I took a chance: I had a dream job as the RSPB's Regional Officer in the Highlands but, as we became more successful, more staff were taken on and the message from HQ became more insistent: I was the manager and working on budgets was more important than the red kite project or any fieldwork. I recognised a worrying trend – the discussion of ecological restoration with the owner of a large estate would be delegated to a new employee straight from college, while people like me were expected to stay at our desks. I decided to be self-employed.

To make sure ecological restoration is really effective on the increasing numbers of rewilding sites, we need more competent and confident ecologists. The apparent acceptance that office-based science will deliver good outcomes must be challenged. I am still doing a lot of fieldwork and it worries me that I meet few professional nature conservationists out doing the same. There's a tendency to use volunteers to do that bit, and even to take casual records from anyone, to fit the bill. We need our best people out there – working, persuading, encouraging and helping get projects underway and keeping them running well. This needs to be job creation on a large scale, for the task is immense.

And yes, it might start with opening gates, but it continues with opening minds, gaining confidences and making lasting friendships, meaning that more of us can join the work to protect our cherished but damaged planet.

When it's gone, it's gone

Working with nature in Scotland, it's difficult to appreciate fully the meaning of extinction. There is no doubt that it might be risky for animals of a particular species to live in a very small range or very specialised habitat, but that doesn't necessarily pose a serious risk to the species as a whole. Way back in the early 1960s, when I was the warden at the Fair Isle Bird Observatory, I did an interview over the phone with Peter Scott, the famous ornithologist. Mine was just a segment of a half-hour BBC radio programme about rare birds at risk of extinction around the world. His question to me was: 'Will the Fair Isle wren go extinct?' This wren is a recognised subspecies living just on that one small island, but it wasn't really at risk, it was just rare. In 1964, my assistant Cliff Waller and I counted the all-time record of fifty-two singing males; numbers then fluctuated between forty and fifty pairs, with no room for any more, but reached a low point of ten pairs in 1981. Even now, sixty years later, there is still a population of between twenty and forty territories. Birders walking round above the cliffs in the spring can still hear the wren's incredible song bursting forth among the calls of the thronging seabirds.

It's entirely reasonable to suspect that Fair Isle might have been visited by the great auk after the last Ice Age, possibly even as a breeding site. Unfortunately for the species, it was ungainly on land when it came ashore to breed, could not fly and was large and edible, so was at risk when humans, the major apex predator, arrived. Great auks lived in many places, but were killed by humans for meat, eggs and feathers, with the last pair breeding in Britain killed on the island of Papay in Orkney in 1812 and 1813 and the final known breeding site in the world in Iceland in 1844. None have been seen since, except as museum specimens.

There have been losses of breeding species in my lifetime in the United Kingdom but they were of birds often common in mainland Europe. There was a particularly interesting time for birdwatchers in the 1970s, when we had a series of cold springs that encouraged a range of Scandinavian birds to linger and breed in Scotland. Redwings and fieldfares were the most common, but we also found wrynecks, bramblings, red-backed shrikes and, on the mountains, Lapland buntings and shore larks. None of them regularly breed now, but that's not extinction, it's range retraction.

I was once fortunate – or rather, maybe, unlucky – to see a bird species just before it became globally extinct. It was the Cape Verde red kite which, depending on whether you are a 'splitter' or a 'lumper', was either a distinctive species, *Milvus fasciicauda*, living on those isolated islands off the west coast of Africa, or just a noticeably different-looking and isolated subspecies, *Milvus milvus fasciicauda*, of the much commoner red kite, *Milvus milvus*, of Europe.

The Cape Verde islands also have populations of breeding ospreys, peregrine falcons and common buzzards, as well as two different island kestrels. One of my raptor friends, Sabine Hille, was carrying out doctoral studies on the kestrels, and in the following years did intensive studies on all the raptor species and the rare endemic Razo lark. She arranged for me to make a short visit to the islands to help trap the kestrels for ringing and biometrics, while at the same time I could check out the breeding ospreys of this isolated archipelago. I was eager to get to know ospreys living in very different habitats to those I knew in Scotland.

When I visited the archipelago, the red kites lived on Santo Antão, an amazing rocky, volcanic island, forty-three kilometres long and twenty-five kilometres wide and rising to nearly 2,000 metres. It was the most north-westerly of the archipelago, with the north-facing coasts broken up by green and cultivated valleys, slopes and ravines. It was awe-inspiring to cross from the dusty southern side and look down into those valleys, with woodlands and an incredible farming system of terraced agriculture. The mainly coastal villages held a population of nearly 40,000 people, so the island was heavily used for growing many crops, as well as fishing around the coasts. The inhabitants, though, had often been close to starvation and many had emigrated.

During fieldwork on the kestrels, we saw Cape Verde kites on six days between 19th and 28th February 1997. Thumbing through my field notebooks of the time, I see my sketches and notes: the first I saw was over the valleys east of Riberra Grande, three valleys distant. It was soaring with a buzzard and a young Egyptian vulture. 'Definitely a red kite,' I wrote, 'but not as bright as the ones at home and seemed smaller; the fork in the chest-nut tail was obvious and there were pale bars on the upper wing and three primaries were damaged on the right wing – could have been caused by man.' At one stage it landed near a farmhouse, where it was chased by a dog.

There was a different one in the same area the next day; two together on the highest slopes on the 22nd; while on Sunday morning, the 23rd, one flew from the beach and round the church at Riberra Grande. We saw none on our field trips in the mountains or to the southern village of Tarrafal, but on the 26th, one was seen over the usual valleys. On the 28th, we saw two higher up near Lombo Branco and noted that one had a greyer head, suggesting adult plumage and making three different birds seen.

Later that day, hiking the hills above Pinhao, we saw either two or three in the morning and, in the afternoon, definitely three – two circling high around the upper Pinhao slopes while another searched the lower slopes. We might, in fact, have seen four different individuals, and all showed chestnut tails. When looking closely at one individual, soaring close to the ground, we noted its bill was overgrown, putting it at a disadvantage when feeding. This may have been a result of a very small inbreeding population.

Catching kestrels involved a lot of sitting around on hillsides watching the traps, but it gave us time to watch the landscape for other raptors, as well as talk about how to save the Cape Verde red kite, for it was a distinctive-looking raptor. The islanders were undoubtedly hostile to the birds because they swooped around the scattered cottages in search of food, and we were told that newly hatched chickens were at risk if the mother hen had taken her brood out onto open land. I'd heard similar stories from long ago in Scotland. We talked about the possibility of increasing food availability for the birds, for it seemed scarce, maybe releasing breeding guinea fowls or providing carrion as substitute food for kites, but the prognosis was not good. In 2001, I returned for another visit to Santo Antão, but by then the Cape Verde red kite was extinct.

A year later, a conservation group made an attempt to save the 'species' by trapping five birds in the eastern islands of Boa Vista and Maio and sending them to England for captive breeding. Sabine and I later examined them there and, embarrassingly for the trappers, they were clearly black kite-type individuals, quite unlike the Cape Verde red kites we had seen in Santo Antão. I suppose extinction was inevitable because, in just over 500 years, the arrival by boat of Portuguese settlers had devastated the original vegetation of savannah woodland, tall shrub and native grassland. The effects of goats, fires and conversion to agriculture had dramatically changed all the islands, as humans tried to sustain an increasing population. Those same humans sometimes trapped and killed kites, while poisoned baits set to kill feral dogs and cats indirectly killed the birds as well.

The Cape Verde red kite was presumably descended from long-lost migrant red kites from Europe. When that happened, no one knows, but however long ago it was, those birds would have been living in a very different and original natural landscape. It's risky to live on small islands, especially when the original habitats, which made them a suitable home, have been utterly destroyed.

Sea eagles:
shooting the messenger

Every now and then, another row blows up over sea eagles in the Western Highlands and Islands of Scotland. The eagles, it's said, are destroying the livelihoods of farmers and crofters who keep sheep. The wildlife people don't believe the numbers of viable lambs that are said to have been killed, while the shepherds don't believe outsiders who, they say, don't know what they are talking about. Decades ago, the Scottish government thought they would get rid of the confrontation by handing out money, but if one looks at claims for livestock losses to wildlife worldwide, whether real or inflated, a compensation system is unsatisfactory. The money offered is never enough and country people know that strenuous complaints usually result in officials backing down and somehow finding more money. Evidence of killing is difficult to obtain, but when the government finds it easier to agree with the complainants, treating possible and probable losses as real losses, the situation goes from bad to worse. The row inevitably leads to bad press and politicians of any hue, with four-year terms in office, are never unaware of the ballot box.

Quite often, complaints about sea eagles will include mention of ancestors 'who didn't have these problems', suggesting that life was much easier when sea eagles were absent or could be killed. Humans exterminated the last of the original Scottish sea eagles in the first years of the 20th century. Unfortunately, very little attention is paid to the dramatic and devastating changes that have taken place in agriculture in these areas in the past century. Some of the most detailed and pertinent research outlining the difficulties of farming and crofting in the Western

Highlands is contained in Frank Fraser Darling's *West Highland Survey* (Oxford University Press, 1955).

As a grandfather, looking back over my life, I have seen crofting and hill farming from 1959 onwards, when it was probably at its zenith for the benefit of the rural community. On Fair Isle that year, while a warden at the famous Bird Observatory, I immersed myself in crofting – I loved the way of life and it was a privilege to make friends with the crofting community. Back in Strathspey for the four years from 1960 to 1963, I was again close to crofters and hill farmers. Their land was carefully and competently worked in traditional ways, aimed at always having 'the land in good heart'. It was hard, relentless work and there was little time to be away from the holding, but there was a pride in milking cows by hand as well as in making butter and cheese. The basis of the year was rotational cropping, with oats, turnips, tatties and hay. There were usually hens and ducks for eggs and meat, hives of bees for the sale of heather honey to city folk up on holiday, and sheep on the common grazing for sale and home killing. Firewood and peats were there for the effort, as was the occasional deer. It was very self-sufficient but all relied on the historical efforts of their ancestors.

When early humans colonised the Highlands, the first land to be cultivated were the slopes at altitudes above the big forests, for there the trees were smaller and needed less physical effort to remove, while the slopes allowed natural draining. The Scotsman John Muir wrote about breaking in farmland in Wisconsin, USA, as a twelve-year-old boy, the eldest son on the family farm of 120 acres of wilderness claimed by his father and named Fountain Lake Farm in 1849. He recalled the day-after-day slog to fell trees, burn brash, uproot big tree stumps and make the soil fertile to grow crops, often rising at 4am and not getting to bed until 9pm. There were Sundays off for exploring, hunting and seeing nature, but after five years the land was exhausted and the wheat crop fell from twenty-five bushels an acre down to five. After eight years, his father bought more land four miles away and their incredible labours started again. Whether in the States or in our own country, these pioneers were the ones who put in the backbreaking work, unaware that their hard graft was a gift to future generations. In Scotland, evidence of the earliest efforts of claiming land goes back millennia, with the still visible huge rocks laid down to form the boundaries.

Throughout most of the time of human presence in the Western Highlands and Islands, the seas were the people's life-blood – they provided the transport links, fish and shellfish for food and seaweed for fertiliser. Patches of good fertile soils were scarce and most farmed land had to be claimed from woodland and improved over time with manure from cattle and seaweed from the shore, as well as careful use of limestone to grow crops. The small native cattle were key to this economy and the dung from those over-wintered in byres created the distinctive middens, from where it was spread on the land every year. During the summers, the cattle were herded to the hills and centuries of transhumance fertilised the hill pastures. This very goodness was snatched from the residents by the incoming shepherds of the Clearances. It's pertinent now to reflect on the people of Dingwall in the 1790s trying to turn back the first flocks of big sheep from the Scottish Borders. They knew the sheep were not in their interests.

The underlying rocks of the west are generally unproductive for agriculture, despite some fertile pockets, and the optimum form of low-intensive farming we saw in the 1950s and 1960s was the result of generations of Highlanders and Islanders husbanding the land so diligently following the back-breaking work of their ancestors. In late September 1960, I drove by road from

Strathspey to Durness and then on to Thurso, and at every township I passed the oats had been cut and stooked in neat rows to dry in the fields. The meadow hay of summer was in ricks at the back of the houses and the potato rigs were still in the ground. Most holdings had a few house cows for milking and the sight of a grey Fergie tractor was becoming common. I lived again on Fair Isle from 1963 to 1970 and wintered in the Highlands; big changes were clearly starting to take place all over the crofting counties.

The old ploughing grant of wartime was stopped. The first of the agricultural chemicals came into use. On Fair Isle, the islanders traditionally kept back good oats for seed each year, but by 1959 the first treated seed came in from the merchants. 'Much better than that you can grow', treated with pink-dusted insecticides to kill problems where none existed and after sowing in the spring, we saw the local twites stumbling about in the fields and dying from pesticide poisoning. Even worse were the insecticides invented in wartime, like DDT. In no time the sheep were being dipped with chemicals such as dieldrin to kill ticks. Often the dippers were close to hill burns for ease of filling and flushing. Dead sheep on the hills were scavenged by golden eagles, and scientists found evidence that the organo-chlorines were depressing breeding and ultimately their numbers. It was a salutary wake-up call for humans who also ate the sheep and in time it was banned. In those years we conservationists got many an earful from irate shepherds for banning their best treatment for ticks.

As the 1970s came in, many changes started to take place. Family crofts that had been going for centuries, had given a good life and livelihood to many generations and sent many a young man or woman out into the world, were being amalgamated as even more young people decided against a farming life. It was hard graft, but there was usually enough food, and there was comradeship, storytelling, music and song. A way of life was changing and the wisdom of a people who had lived through fair weather and bad times was devalued as they were encouraged to be 'real farmers'. The men from the Department encouraged change, in places with little to change. As an old wise farmer in the 1960s said to me: 'These men want us to change, for they are the second sons of Aberdeen-shire farmers. The big fertile farms of Buchan or the Mearns are not Lochaber or Skye.' Fraser Darling's recommendations to farm in sympathy with the land in the *West Highland Survey* were basically binned.

The UK joined the EEC in 1973 and, not long after, attractive European subsidies to keep sheep meant a headlong dash out of cattle, tatties, turnips and often hay. The old husbandry of one cow to one sheep was gone. In 1977 the lime subsidy ceased, meaning that many small hill farms and crofts stopped annual liming. On top of that, there was often no longer any cattle dung to put on the land for rotational cropping. For many, these were good years when sheep was a great cash crop, but those sheep were exhausting the 'good heart' of the land. This was not new: the same had happened following the great sheep bonanza of the 19th century, when production of lambs and wool was exceptional on the cattle-evicted rich pastures. But as the 20th century wore on, despite improvements in veterinary medicines and treatments, sheep farming was not bringing in the same profits, despite subsidies. Even the wool from blackface sheep was now penny poor compared to pre-artificial fibre times. It's hard now to remember when we bought our first fleece jacket without a sheep involved, but it was in the latter half of my life.

By the end of the 20th century, all sorts of grants had ceased and EU subsidies started to change. More recently, payments were decoupled from the actual numbers of livestock and term-limited Single Farm Payments came in, while the numbers of sheep in north-west Scotland tumbled. The people remaining in farming and crofting on marginal lands were finding that their farming activities were less economic, while everything else became more expensive. The old ways of keeping the land 'in good heart', as required in many a lease, were mainly gone. Bigger tractors ploughed fields and spread artificial fertilisers, and anyone who has paid a contract tractor man knows that his main aim is to get back out the gate as fast as possible. Deep ploughing was unsuitable for these fragile ancient, often human-made, soils – they became waterlogged, true soil fertility declined and the bonny fields of oats and hay of the 1960s often became overrun by hard rush.

I crofted for about fifteen years in Strathspey. I loved having suckler cows and their calves, hiring a bull from the Department, ploughing, harrowing and sowing oats while avoiding the lapwing and oystercatcher nests with eggs, although I never liked sheep as I did cattle. Enjoying the craic with neighbours, with George the vet, and at marts in Kingussie or Grantown. Eating our own eggs and wether lamb, cutting peats and logs, and sharing our way of life with friends and visitors to the croft, but knowing there was the safety net of a monthly salary from my wildlife career. And I remember 'picking stones', for every year's ploughing brought to the surface more boulders and stones, all to be lifted by hand and dumped at the field boundaries.

In January 2020, a retired keeper asked me to show him and his older son an historic stone on the hill farm where I spent many a day cultivating, cutting and baling hay. We agreed a time and drove up into the top fields. I was shocked and deeply saddened at what I found there, for the four big fields were covered in rushes. It's a mistake for people to think, blithely, that if you stop cultivating, these poor soils will become wildflower meadows. Fraser Darling once said of agriculture on poor land: 'Taken from the forest mistakenly for agriculture, they should return to woodland,' but that doesn't immediately salve my pain at being beaten by rushes. This despair of trying to farm in a changed world in which prices fail to keep up, people are eating less meat, regulations are increasingly complicated and the public objects to subsidising farmers means that their lives are unrecognisably different from those lived by their grandfathers.

Farm abandonment, a lack of active cultivation and mixed agriculture and the over-grazing of marginal lands have happened in many countries of Europe; and the smallholdings that sustained families through generations, without outside support, are in general a thing of the past. In a scenario such as this, those involved in sheep rearing feel oppressed even before they voice complaints about sea eagles in Scotland, lynx in Norway or wolves in the French mountains. As a country person reared on a part-time smallholding in the 1940s and '50s, I feel sorry for them and can understand the frustration when the person who investigates their complaints will be on a secure and comfortable salary. The real problems are dropping profitability, increasing and chaotic rainfall and declining soil fertility. If every last sea eagle and golden eagle were removed from Scotland, there would still be no return to a really profitable self-supporting sheep economy in the less-favoured areas. The complaints about eagles are, in many ways, a messenger, drawing our attention to the decline and abandonment of hard-won soils. And we know that to shoot the messenger is really to miss the point.

Sixty years of ospreys

It is 8th April 2020, and it's exactly sixty years since one of the most important days of my life.

In 1960, I was just a week into my new work as a warden at the RSPB's Operation Osprey at Loch Garten in the Scottish Highlands. Each day, we waited for the pair's arrival after their previous year's successful rearing of three young. It was a very exciting time but also an anxious one, for these ospreys were the only nesting pair in the British Isles.

Friday 8th April 1960 was cold and grey, and it was raining on my early visit to the still-empty nest. I returned to the forward hide in the early afternoon, checked the eyrie with my binoculars, then scanned the old trees dotted across the peat mosses. There he was, perched on a branch of an ancient pine, preening his wet feathers. To me, he was fantastic – he had just winged in from a 3,500-mile migration flight from Africa. 'After an hour of preening,' I wrote in my diary, 'he carried a dead stick to the nest at 3.35pm, and in quick succession five more, snapped in flight from nearby trees. He rearranged his old nest before leaving to fish at 3.50pm.' I hurried back to our camp to phone the news to my boss, George Waterson, at the RSPB in Edinburgh.

We had a ten-day wait until the female arrived, and the pair went on to rear two more young for the fledgling osprey population in Scotland. They were seen that year by thousands of visitors to Loch Garten, probably the world's first public viewing site of a rare breeding bird in the dawn of eco-tourism. It was also the start of my life's involvement with these beautiful fish-eating raptors, which have contributed so greatly to my enjoyment of – and involvement in – nature. I had planned to visit Loch Garten on the exact anniversary date and walk up that long, familiar track to view the ancient nest tree, now long-dead but still standing, with the present osprey eyrie in the tree next door. Loch Garten, though, is out-of-bounds in the first worrying days of lockdown. I am fortunate that I will likely see an osprey passing our house today instead, from one of the local eyries.

Early this morning, on my laptop, courtesy of a webcam, I watched the female on a nest at Poole Harbour, in Dorset. She reminded me of the male at the Loch Garten nest in April 1960 as she stared up into the skies, looking for her mate – hopefully the male she met last summer – coming in from West Africa. He is a bird we translocated from the Rutland Water population to Poole Harbour in 2017, himself descended from ospreys moved to Rutland Water from nests in northern Scotland.

And so the osprey year continues while I watch, remotely. All I need is an all-clear to travel and I will make a pilgrimage to that special Scots pine at Loch Garten, where so much of what I have worked and lived for began, sixty years ago.

Green bridges

In the late 1980s I regularly drove from my home in Strathspey to the RSPB office at Munlochy on the Black Isle. Nearly every morning there was some dead creature on the road, run over and killed by a vehicle, mostly during the hours of darkness. Roe deer were occasional casualties, along with brown hare, mountain hare, rabbits, red squirrel, badger and fox, with red deer on the higher sections. On top of those casualties were scavengers – such as black-headed gull, common gull, lesser black-backed gull, buzzard and crow – which had themselves been struck while eating a flattened roadkill.

At one stage, a new dualled section was built between Daviot and Moy, south of Inverness. It cut through forestry plantations where there was a population of sika deer. The ones living close to the new fast road were soon killed out. Similarly, the dualling of a longer length of the A9 trunk road south of Drumochter ran either side of a wide central reservation of natural vegetation, which attracted red deer. Speeding lorries and other vehicles were soon colliding with and killing red deer, often with serious risks for the drivers.

The improvements to the A9 trunk road involved planners with a love of long, sweeping curves that followed the contours, with not a single green bridge for nature in sight. I recently saw the first designs for the dualling of the A96 trunk road in Moray and, again, there was no provision at all for green bridges. In fact, when I rack my brain, I cannot point to a single green bridge anywhere in my ken. There may be a few underpasses that allow wildlife to pass beneath the road, but I don't think any of these were designed as wildlife underpasses: they were an accidental benefit where a road crossed a river or an access road was left.

When I have been driving in countries elsewhere in the world – in Germany, for example – I've noticed really effective green bridges and green underpasses for nature. The roads are deer-fenced and animals are encouraged to move along to the next safe route. In other countries, such as Norway and China, the use of multiple road tunnels, instead of sweeping contour routes, obviates the need for these measures, for the land above the tunnel forms a truly massive green pathway.

The design and provision of green bridges and underpasses has been an encouraging innovation in terms of limiting damage to wildlife and improving driver safety. It's disappointing, then, that the UK is so far behind in the building of nature-friendly crossing places. They must be mandatory for all new fast roads if we are to get rid of our blackspots for wildlife deaths.

Saving the California condor

May 2019 marked the hatching of the 1,000th chick in the California Condor Recovery Program; this one was at a wild nest in the Zion National Park in south-west Utah. It was a remarkable milestone in the recovery 'from the dead' of this hugely impressive black-and-white vulture. After four and a half months, on 25th September 2019, the bird, named 1K, flew from its cliff nest site for the first time. It was the first success for its parents; the female had hatched in 2006 at San Diego Zoo and the male had hatched at Boise, Idaho, three years later. Both had been released into the wild at Vermilion Cliffs, on the north side of the Grand Canyon in Arizona. In May 2020, the youngster was identified at Vermilion Cliffs and live-trapped by the Peregrine Fund condor team. It was given a quick health check, weighed and fitted with a wing tag and a satellite transmitter. Two days later it was back at Zion with its parents, meaning it flew about fifty kilometres in that forty-eight-hour period, but that's just a short flight for a condor.

In February 2008, my wife and I were privileged to meet the condor team at Vermilion Cliffs. On 27th February we drove north from the superb landscape of Organ Pipe Cactus National Monument in southern Arizona, through the huge prairies of Navajo County and finally turned west off the highway. Thankfully, after a very long day's drive, we found Chris Parish and his Peregrine Fund crew. Before dark, we returned to the bridge over the river and were shown six condors, two near-adult males and four immature male birds, which at dusk flew to roost on the bridge.

Next morning was the start of one of the special days of my life, spent watching and learning about condors. We followed Chris along the road below the cliffs to the viewpoint, looking across dry grassland and sage bush to the dramatic line of red cliffs, some 500 feet high. Fourteen condors were patrolling the skies above the ridge, ten-foot wingspans taking them effortlessly back and forth. A raven showed their size but even that at times was lessened by the clarity of the brilliant sunny day and the immensity of the Grand Canyon landscape. Chris took us to a deserted homestead where we met Rob and Maria, while two other members of the crew were on the cliffs. The team was hoping to catch one of the condors and – given that eating deer carcasses shot with lead bullets was a major hazard for condors – I learnt about an amazing procedure, a bit like dialysis, by which they could lessen the lead burden in each bird's blood.

We talked as we sat in the sun, gazing at these fantastic birds. I was told that a pair in a canyon forty miles away was almost certainly incubating their single egg but that successful breeding by more condors was proving difficult. I felt sure that would not last, for the first young condors had only been released from captivity twelve years previously. In the afternoon we drove further on to the Kaibab Plateau on the north side of the canyon, but it was covered in deep snow with just the highway clear. Walking up a hill we saw pinyon jays, nutcrackers and mountain bluebirds before returning to the condor base. That evening I gave a talk about our projects on sea eagle, red kite and osprey reintroductions in Europe, as well as on raptor satellite-tracking.

Earlier on during our Arizona visit we had been hosted by Noel and Helen Snyder at their home in Portal near the Nevada/Mexican border. They lived in a fantastic area for birding, but our visit was really a pilgrimage for me to meet Noel again. I had met him briefly in the Scottish Highlands thirty or so years before, when he was preparing for an amazing adventure working with condors that was to transform the fortunes of the bird. Long ago, the great raptor ranged over much of the western United States, north to Canada and – in the earlier eras of the original mega-fauna – probably over much of the States. In South America, the equally impressive Andean condor breeds in much larger numbers.

Many studies took place in the second half of the 20th century and they all pointed to the California condor heading for extinction, with the last population in the coastal ranges of southern California. The species was losing range and population size through the impact of humans, but also through habitat loss (resulting in less carrion), pollution, accidental deaths and illegal persecution. There was great controversy over what to do about the situation, with many differing views on the best way ahead. A request to take two wild birds to test captive breeding was angrily opposed, with some people saying they would rather take a chance on them dying out than have them in captivity. There was even a view that the species should be allowed to die out in dignity.

In 1979, the U.S. Fish and Wildlife Service decided not to give up on the species and set up the California Condor Recovery Program, with the biologist Noel Snyder leading a multi-interest team. They got to work, catching and radio-tracking individual condors, investigating their survival and breeding success and showing that their major problem was the ingestion of lead ammunition when eating deer carcasses killed by hunters. Lead poisoning was killing them: only twenty-two condors were living in the wild and the annual mortality was way above normal. Noel recommended that the wild population be captured before they died, in order to create a captive breeding population. This could lead in the future to a successful return to the wild when environmental conditions were more favourable. He received harsh criticism for his views, but more organisations and individuals started to recognise that this was, without doubt, the only way forward. The recovery team started live-trapping the remaining condors, including taking young from nests in the wild, to join the breeding programme started at San Diego Zoo, and the final wild bird was captured in 1987.

There were many technical problems to overcome with captive breeding and subsequent release, and some of the team's ideas were trialled using the closely similar Andean condor. It was testament to the quality of the work that the first California condors could be released back into the wild in southern California just five years later, in 1992, with other releases at Vermilion Cliffs in Arizona (1996), central California (1997) and in Baja California, Mexico (2002). I guess there would have been some Californians complaining about them being in Arizona. In March 2020, the total world population stood at 518, with 337 wild and free-flying, and 181 still in captive breeding locations.

California recently banned the use of lead bullets for hunting deer, encouraging the swap to non-toxic copper ammunition, and there are other programmes aimed at working with rural and indigenous communities to make the environment safer for condors, taking it as a totem species for nature as a whole. Further releases are also planned by the Yurok tribe in the Pacific Northwest, to restore the species to another part of its ancestral range. My few days with Noel and Helen were special to me, as was our visit with Chris Parish and the guys at the Peregrine Fund. From talking and listening, I recognised that those early years at the end of the 20th century were very tough times for committed conservation people, who were often personally and harshly criticised for their views and actions. They faced hard choices, difficult decisions and fallings-out with colleagues and had to be bold and determined to turn the problem round. I recognised many of the stages of their project as similar to our own wildlife management dilemmas in Scotland. And, writing this, I know that to turn round the extremely worrying misfortunes of the capercaillie and the wildcat will require equally bold and determined conservation management.

Oystercatchers on a cliff edge

'Kleep kleep' … Last night I heard the call of the oystercatchers passing over the house on the first reconnoitre of their summer home. In March they return from their winter quarters to the fields around our home, where they nest. For us, it's one of the really distinctive signs of the coming spring, just beaten by a few weeks by the wild and gorgeous song of the local mistle thrushes, while that much smaller black-and-white bird, the pied wagtail, returns from the south a little later than the oystercatcher. Any day now I will see a male wagtail, in his very smart breeding plumage, perched on the roof of our house, then busily running around the lawn chasing flies.

But it's the oystercatcher that interests me here, for it's the bird that could tell a very interesting story of its association with humans. I first got to know them as common breeding birds on Fair Isle when I was warden at the Bird Observatory. The birds that breed there return from late February through March and stake out their territories from year to year around the island, with most of them nesting in the coastal strip. The sheep-grazed grassland, across the havens on Buness from where we lived, was ideal for them; the short turf was littered with large rocks and jumbles of shattered rocks and gravel, ideal for hiding the eggs in their nests.

Oystercatchers in spring are very noisy, very demonstrative and totally engaging to watch, as the small gangs of brightly coloured displaying birds race around, their bills and legs, just so red at this season, contrasting with their black and white plumage. They will often engage in a communal running display, several pairs together, piping loudly, outdoing each other in noise and action, while their exuberant, slow-motion butterfly display flight is just the epitome of 'Look at me, I'm very fit and an ideal mate'. And then they settle down in individual pairs to breed around the island.

When I lived on Fair Isle, there were about seventy pairs, as well a non-breeding flock of younger birds at the south end of the island. They were summer residents at Fair Isle, migrating south in August to winter in Wales, north-west England and even northern France, where they would join together in large flocks along the big estuaries, roosting together at high tide on shingle points. As the tide went down, they would search the exposed sand and mud for shellfish like cockles and marine worms. Their winters were very social, while in summer they would breed as individual, scattered pairs. The ones I knew on Fair Isle returned, often as long-lived birds. The individual pairs would usually return to the same territories from year to year and often make a nest scrape for their eggs in much the same place. A juvenile ringed on the island in 1983 was found freshly dead on 26th May 2011, just two days short of twenty-eight years, while the oldest on the British Trust for Ornithology's species longevity list is just over forty-one years.

In the 1960s, oystercatchers did well on Fair Isle, for at low tide they could hunt around the island for limpets and other shellfish on the exposed rocks, while on the short grass they used their long bills to probe for worms, leatherjackets and other invertebrates. It had not always been like that for oystercatchers, though, for one of the old islanders told me about the long-line fishing of the olden days. The human population of Fair Isle was much larger, with several hundred islanders eking out a living on an exposed island. They were great fishermen and ventured far out to sea in their six-oared open boats to catch haddock, cod and ling. The long lines were kept in baskets with hundreds of hooks that required baiting every day before being taken to sea. Limpet was a favourite bait to fix on the hooks and that involved daily excursions to the coast at low tide to gather them. By the end of the summer, nearly all the limpets had been gathered and there was no doubt that humans were a conspicuous competitor to the oystercatchers for the birds' favourite prey. When families were big and food was scarce, it's also very likely that oystercatcher eggs were gathered for food, alongside those of gulls and other seabirds, to feed hungry mouths. Nowadays, fewer pairs nest on Fair Isle and their breeding success is poorer, probably due to predation by the increased population of great skuas.

Where I live in the Scottish Highlands, I know the oystercatcher as a summer nesting bird well inland as well as on the coast, or as a common wintering species on the shores of the Moray Firth. Originally they probably spread up the big rivers and nested on the braided river shingles. They would have found the traditional agriculture practised on Highland farms very suitable to their needs, although it's likely that in the first half of the 20th century, as in earlier times, the tradition of collecting gulls' eggs for food and also those of lapwings, which almost certainly included some oystercatcher eggs, would have kept their numbers lower than they might have been. When I was younger, I remember people still gathering lapwing eggs to sell in the markets, but by the late 1960s that old tradition was gone.

As with the lapwing (see 'Losing our lapwings'), changes in agriculture – intensification and the use of chemicals, combined with the abandonment of mixed stock farming – have been detrimental for inland-breeding oystercatchers. Unlike lapwings, which often winter on farmland, the oystercatchers move to the coast, where habitat and food is plentiful.

The poor breeding success, despite the adults living long lives, suggests to me that some year, before too long, the unalloyed joy of hearing 'kleep kleep' in the moonlight – telling me that 'we are home for another year' – will be gone. Unless, of course, we learn how – truly – to restore nature and farm in a more natural and acceptable way. Fortunately for the species, the oystercatcher can still breed successfully around our coasts and on the islands. It will remain a beautiful bird in our lives but will more likely be seen standing on cliff edges than on inland fields. Nature knows that what worked for the bird for a time no longer does. The oystercatcher will have to rely on its more ancient haunts.

Summer

An octogenarian dangling from a rope

At my home in the Highlands of Scotland, tucked safely in a drawer, is a simple wooden pulley. The rope long rotted away, it's a memento of a great man and an extraordinary eagle eyrie, and it reminds me that some of the work we do with wildlife, which we might think of as ground-breaking, has been carried out by others before us.

Forty years ago, I was doing a lot of fieldwork on golden eagles, especially in the glens of north Inverness-shire and Ross-shire. I knew I was missing a nesting pair in Glen Affric and could not find where they were breeding. There was a lovely period of weather in early May, so I hiked up through the woods one early evening, allowing me to scan the whole glen in the lovely evening light. That night I bivvied under a tree near the top of the glen, so that I was on my way soon after dawn, searching the woods. I disturbed an eagle from a group of old Scots pines, so I walked into the group of great trees. Droppings, pellets, moulted feathers, fresh down and some red grouse feathers told me immediately that I was in the right place, and that eagles had been using the wood regularly for roosting. Another hundred metres further on I looked up into an ancient Caledonian pine and saw the huge nest I'd been looking for.

It was a golden eagle eyrie that was not on our maps, and it was in use. I was really pleased that I had filled in a missing part of the jigsaw of contiguous home ranges in the Inverness glens. But when I got to the bottom of the tree and looked up, I saw to my amazement that the nest was built on top of big spars of timber. Who had built this nest? When? And why?

I sought out my friend Don, the forest ranger, and after racking his brains he remembered that in the 1930s, when he'd been a boy, the legendary eagle-watcher Seton Gordon had called on his father, who worked on the estate. Seton had known that eagles' eyrie for some years and had just found that the main branch had broken under its weight, sending the nest to the ground. With the help of the locals, they had fixed in two big spars to replace the broken limb and rebuilt the nest. Since that summer, it had been in use, on and off, for half a century.

Some months later, I returned with two friends to ring the eaglet. We found, hanging above the nest, the original wooden pulley used to pull up the timber. A few summers later, on another visit to the eyrie, I found the pulley on the ground, as its rope had finally rotted. I put it in my pocket, a precious souvenir.

But it's not a souvenir of times past. That story has been repeated, in various forms, in various places, throughout my working life.

In September 2020, golden eagles were reported to be breeding successfully for the first time in living memory at the Dundreggan reserve, owned by the charity Trees for Life. The story soon became news worldwide, but it had begun ten years earlier.

On 30th June 2010, I had driven north with David Clark and Ryan Munroe, of Alladale Wilderness Reserve, to the RSPB Forsinard Reserve in the Flow Country. The manager, Norrie Russell, took us some of the way in a cross-country Argocat before we walked across the hills to an eagle nest with two big young. We were there to fit satellite transmitters, as part of our eagle studies. The eyrie was on a small cliff overlooking the typical Flow Country landscape of peaty lochans dotted across a vast area of deep peats. We ringed both young before returning them to their eyrie, transmitter 57107 on the young male, 57106 on the female. We had a great walk back in the evening sun and I finally got home at midnight after a wonderful day's fieldwork.

The male eaglet left his parents and his natal home in October and ranged widely, but the female stayed with her parents until after the New Year. During his wanderings, the male arrived at Dundreggan on 17th November 2010 and roosted there overnight in a cliff, before heading north the following day. This is part of Glen Moriston, which runs north and west of Loch Ness. It was an area I knew well in the late 1970s and 1980s when I monitored golden eagles in the Highlands. In those days, though, the glen was a blackspot for the illegal persecution of large raptors, so the ancient breeding sites were unoccupied. By 2008, Dundreggan Estate had been purchased by Trees for Life, during a period when I was one of their volunteer board members.

During the collection of satellite data from over twenty eagles, I had noted that many chose to visit long-abandoned nesting areas, and this led to my suggesting to Alan Featherstone Watson, the founder of Trees for Life, that we build a nest on the new reserve. In October 2015, I went to Dundreggan and explained to the staff how to build an eagle nest, before we headed to the site. Using my binoculars, I searched the line of low cliffs from a distance and saw one place that looked suitable for building an eyrie. It also matched the GPS location on my map of the eagle's overnight stay in 2010. Alan had asked a local climber, Ewan, to come with his climbing gear, and after fixing ropes, he and I abseiled into the best ledge. To my amazement, the overgrown ledge contained the ancient stick remains of an eagle eyrie, probably from the middle of the last century. I cleared the ledge of vegetation, including a small conifer that was blocking access, before we hauled up bundles of sticks tied to our rope by the group of helpers below. Arranging the sticks, adding moss and grass and, finally, a topping of leaf litter resulted in a good starter eyrie for prospecting eagles.

Doug Gilbert, the manager of the reserve, reported an eagle over the cliff that winter but it was not until August 2020 that I heard the exciting news that a pair was rearing a single eaglet in our nest. He reported that they had built a big structure on top of our original nest and it is very likely that they had started taking an interest in the ancient breeding site the year before.

This is an exciting development and demonstrates that eagles will successfully return to ancient nesting places when illegal persecution is stopped. Sometimes they do it by themselves, and sometimes they do it with our help. I love that these big raptors build up histories, with eyries used for centuries and some individuals living very long lives. Five years may seem a long time to wait for successful breeding, but we have built nests in other good places and are still waiting for them to be occupied.

For Trees for Life, it is a tribute to their management of their rewilding reserve, and there's every likelihood that this pair will decide to stay and become regular successful breeders. The global interest was very encouraging and gave us a chance to point out that the success of this pair is part of the ecological restoration of degraded lands: this nest is an icon of restoring nature. And it's created some great headlines – my son-in-law messaged me to say that he particularly liked the caption below one of the newspaper photos, describing me as 'an octogenarian conservationist dangling from a rope'.

Nature's woodworkers

The simplest things, which all of us can see whenever we walk through woodland, can tell us the biggest things about evolution on our planet. Take woodpecker holes. Just as a woodworker might select the right drill bit for a particular job, nature provides a range of different sized woodpeckers, making different sized holes in trees. At one end of the scale in Europe are the tiny lesser spotted woodpeckers, making holes of just three centimetres in diameter, while large black woodpeckers have a nest hole of more than three times that in diameter. I'm not sure that you can talk about altruism in the animal world, but someone should tell the woodpeckers how special they are as a keystone species.

There used to be a distinctive clump of dead Scots pine trees near where I lived in Abernethy Forest in the Scottish Highlands. I think they had died because a little river nearby had become blocked, the water spreading out to create a small marsh around their bases, finally killing them. They reminded me of similar clumps of dead trees in beaver-dammed ponds elsewhere. Looking across the hundred metres or so to this group of trees, it was clear that the trees were dotted with great spotted woodpecker nest holes. This is a species once thought to be extinct in Scotland, a note in the Victorian-era bird books suggesting that there may have been just a tiny population of less than a handful of pairs hanging on in that very same Abernethy Forest. But things have changed since then.

These present-day holes were always worth a look in spring and early summer, for as well as finding young woodpeckers calling loudly from their nest, I could discover one or two of the old holes being used for breeding by swifts. It was absolutely lovely to watch and hear them dashing through the open forest and across the bogs, swooping up and into one of the old holes. Twice in the 1970s, a very rare breeding species called the wryneck also chose to live there, for they like to lay their eggs in vacant woodpecker holes. One year there was just a single male perching at the very top of the dead trees, incessantly giving its 'pee-pee-pee' call, while in another year a pair of wryneck nested.

Before swifts lived in the roofs of our buildings and became a familiar sight in towns and villages, their original haunts would have been holes in trees, often excavated by woodpeckers. Many years ago, when the famous cameraman Hugh Miles was making a film with the RSPB on the birds of the native pinewood, he was filming, from his hide, a pair of great spotted woodpeckers feeding their young in a nest hole in the same forest. Their red-topped heads stuck out, waiting for the food-carrying parents, and what a noise they made! He filmed on the day that the young woodpeckers fledged and left their nest chamber, and was amazed that, within very little time at all, a pair of swifts flew down and dived into the hole. The swifts must reconnoitre the forests, checking out dead trees and almost certainly selecting the holes being used to rear that season's brood of woodpeckers. These will be the best nest sites, with possibly the lowest burden of parasites.

Holes in trees, as well as being really important nesting and roosting sites for a variety of bird species, are also important for mammals such as bats and invertebrates such as bees and wasps. In the ancient forests before man made an impact, cutting down trees for timber and firewood, there were of course many more non-excavated holes caused by damage and disease during the lifetime of individual trees. Some of those would have been major cavities, capable of holding bat roosts, breeding tawny owls and even larger creatures. The cavities in those eras may have outnumbered woodpecker holes but nowadays, in our managed woodlands, natural holes are surprisingly scarce, meaning that woodpecker holes are very important. They also last for many years and plenty are available for use for several decades.

Nowadays, in Britain, we can get over the lack of holes by building and erecting nest boxes of all shapes and sizes and with hole sizes carefully tailored to the species of interest. In the 1960s, I put up large nest boxes to encourage goldeneye ducks to breed in Scotland, which led to me meeting ornithologists in Sweden who were studying the same species. Many of their birds, though, were breeding in the holes created by black woodpeckers. I remember being amazed when one of my Swedish friends pointed to a hole in a live aspen that must have been sixty feet above the ground. It was regularly used by goldeneye, and the young ducklings must have had an exciting first view of the outside world as they jumped out and floated to the ground.

That first visit to the northern forests also showed me places where different species of owls were nesting in different sized woodpecker holes. One tree I will always remember was a live Norway spruce with two small woodpecker holes, one at about a metre from the ground, the other one twice as high. My friend smiled and told me that, in years of deep snow, a pygmy owl would use the higher one, while in years of less snow it might use the lower one.

Woodpeckers generally make a new nest each year, which is beneficial to the other birds that use these nest cavities, with a supply of new nest holes always available. This is almost certainly important from the point of view of predation, for many of these hole-nesting birds can be predated by pine martens in the larger holes, and by stoats and weasels in the lower, smaller ones. The people in Sweden that I met in 1979, when the small population of goldeneye ducks breeding in my nest boxes in Strathspey was increasing, told me that the worst predator was the pine marten, which at that time was absent from my study area. In their studies on the goldeneyes using black woodpecker holes, they found that nearly three-quarters of the nests in the new woodpecker holes were successful, but that only one third succeeded in nest holes that had been around for several years. Now that the martens have again spread across Scotland, I understand clearly what they were talking about. The martens certainly learn and remember the location of nest boxes, to raid them for eggs or young, even killing the adult ducks. Move the boxes around into new places each spring, though, and the ducks have a greater chance of success.

Black woodpeckers are common in the woods of mainland Europe but have never crossed the Channel to colonise the British Isles, so big woodpecker hole nesting sites are not available in our country for larger birds like stock doves and jackdaws. They need to find non-excavated sites, but over a dozen species – including starling, redstart, nuthatch and various tits – nest in the old cavities made by the three British-occurring woodpeckers. Starlings have decreased and the lack of competition for nest sites is thought to be one of the reasons great spotted woodpeckers are doing so well, but I have always suspected that it is the woodpeckers' love of fat balls and nut feeders in gardens which have boosted winter survival. In my younger days, there were no fat balls hung in gardens and no visiting woodpeckers, which had to work for a living, searching the woods to find enough food to survive the winters rather than joining the list of species eating 'feeder food'. Since the 1970s, the population of great spots has gone up by 300 per cent or more, and the species even started to colonise Ireland in 2008.

The rapidly increasing population of great spotted woodpeckers has also increased predation on the nestlings of hole-nesting birds. The woodpeckers bash their way into nest boxes or nesting holes to extract young tits to carry off to feed their own offspring, while they also predate much rarer and declining species such as lesser spotted woodpeckers and willow tits. They are a bold and aggressive species but do themselves get predated by martens in the north. The young are safer if the nest hole is firm and not easily attacked, and the nest cavity deep and beyond the reach of the marten's front paws.

When I hear of these raids, such as the one on three tit boxes in next-door's garden, I think of myself as a nest raider when I was young. I must have been about ten years old when, with my pals, I climbed a big elm to a green woodpecker's nest. I was eager to take an egg for my collection, in the days before that was illegal. I went home and, without my mum knowing, took a long-handled silver spoon. I tied it to a stick and, with the spoon end bent over, tried to lift out an egg. The spoon fell off and disappeared into the cavity. I was in deep trouble; my hand was just too big to fish it out, so I had to make another trip home for a saw to enlarge the hole, retrieve the spoon and take an egg. I felt so guilty about raiding the nest and still do, but I certainly learnt how well made woodpeckers' holes are.

It's incredible how woodpeckers can construct these amaz-ing nesting cavities, even in living trees; special cushioning and muscles prevent them from damaging their brains. The first bit must be hard enough, chiselling into a live tree, using the strong muscles in the neck to create an entrance hole just big enough to squeeze through – six centimetres for a green woodpecker. But then the bird has to change direction and drill down vertically inside the trunk, getting rid of the chips as it goes. It takes several weeks or even more to complete, for the internal chamber must be nearly fifty centimetres deep as well as nearly twenty centimetres in diameter. It's a truly mammoth task for a bird.

I would love to see more holes in trees and reduce the need for artificial nest boxes, but although I've searched, I've never found a satisfactory tool that could replicate the activities of woodpeckers.

Would it not be great if we could make one? Some American ornithologists did work out a different way of creating nest holes for one of their rarer woodpeckers, but in no way did it come up to the standard of the bird's. When I think of the ability of humans to drill for oil thousands of feet under the sea and then change the direction of the drilling bit to get to the oil reservoir, I recognise technological ingenuity. Surely some one could invent a 'woodpecker hole maker'? Our uniform plantations could be given a face-lift for hole-nesting birds and allow a much greater number of holes, outwitting even the martens.

Grazing and range management

Written during a field visit to northern Iceland in late August 1988, showing my growing concerns for ecological restoration over thirty years ago.

A few weeks ago, I sat on a hill above a river in northern Iceland. The slopes to the west of me rose gently to 2,000 feet. They were barren, except for a three-acre field of green grass set in a desert of grey cinders and grit, criss-crossed by erosion gullies. People would marvel at man's ability to win this small, fenced field from the wilderness, yet the true story was that once the whole hillside had been green. This field was, in fact, the last vestige. Several centuries of overgrazing by sheep had destroyed the native vegetation, continued grazing had caused erosion scars and the wind, finally, had blown away the topsoil.

Below me, in the river, were small islands protected from grazing and covered with lush growth, especially of willows. On our way to the hill, we had talked to a farmer turning hay. His forty or so acres of meadows were green and fertile, producing excellent hay to winter his 500 sheep. This farm's rough grazing was in good condition. The sheep numbers were not too high and the only noticeable effect was an absence of willow, one of the first bushes to be eaten out by sheep. In stark contrast, a mile or so to the east, there was a similar-sized farm with its hay meadow surrounded by a desert of stones. The old fences and stone dykes, naked in the wind, outlined fields of yesteryear. This was the erosion front and the farm would soon be deserted.

It is believed that when the Vikings first settled in Iceland from Scandinavia in the ninth century, sixty per cent of the land surface was vegetated, usually with scrub woodland of birch and willow. Cattle, sheep and horses have been man's traditional grazing animals. The sheep, in particular, were kept inside in winter but were free to roam the uplands all summer. Iceland's geology has always made it subject to dramatic natural events – the action of ice, and of volcanoes, for example – but the overgrazing by sheep, especially in recent centuries, has resulted in serious damage to the surface of the land. Once the vegetative layer is broken, wind and water can carry away thousands of years' worth of topsoil. In the end, the land is as bare as when the glaciers had just gone. Today, only twenty-five per cent of Iceland is vegetated, a loss of thirty-five per cent in ten centuries.

In a hostile climate like Iceland, nature is unforgiving. Man and nature both suffer the consequences of any mistakes. Iceland is trying hard to combat erosion: the Soil Conservation Service is fencing areas and trying to halt the erosion front by means of artificial fertilisers and seeding, even spraying them from the air, but the major requirement is to persuade farmers to reduce the numbers of sheep on rough grazings and, in many areas, to remove them altogether. Much of the land is lost – in fact, a staggering three and a half million hectares has been degraded since man and his animals arrived – and they have a long hard road to travel even to prevent further losses.

The Scottish Highlands do not have glaciers or active volcanoes but there are many similarities with Iceland. Long ago much of our land was covered by forest and deciduous scrubland. Centuries of exploitation, burning and clearing have dramatically changed the face of the Highlands. Large numbers of sheep in the last two centuries and, more recently, red deer have degraded much of the uplands. Large-scale burning, especially on hilly areas of high rainfall, has contributed to erosion and environmental degradation. Unlike Iceland, our soils do not blow away in a dramatic manner, but high rainfall erodes and degrades in its own way, and the waterlogged land becomes ever poorer.

Nature's original vegetation provided the best chance of increasing the quality of soil cover and promoting optimum diversity of plant and animal life. Sheep and deer overgrazing on the open hill decrease this diversity, as they seek out all the most succulent plants first. The long-term trend is to poor quality grasses and sedges with very little being put back into the soil. These long-term extractive processes are serious and, like every other country in the world, we need to be conscious of the need for soil conservation. Our land needs to be in the best possible heart. Present-day management should not be allowed to compromise the long-term future.

Hill farmers need help to change the pattern of grazing. It often needs to be closer to that of past times: fewer sheep, fewer deer, more cattle and more deciduous woodland and scrub. The aim should be soil and vegetation improvement leading to a healthier grazing range and a considerable enhancement in wildlife communities and scenic beauty.

*

IT'S 2021, THIRTY-THREE YEARS LATER, and I have just Googled 'Iceland and land restoration' and it's encouraging that the Soil Conservation Service, Forest Service, universities and the Icelandic people have been working hard on the problem. The symbiosis between planted downy birch and Nootka lupin has proved particularly successful, and these pioneers are then colonised by woolly willow. An extra 130 square kilometres of woodland have been established since the 1990s and dust storm events have been greatly reduced. Under the most serious examples of desertification, Iceland has demonstrated a determination for ecological restoration.

Morven's son

Some ospreys remain in my mind for many years. There are old favourites like Logie, the first that I tracked with a new and highly accurate GPS satellite transmitter in 2007. Another was her neighbour, who became known as Morven, who'd tried to take over Logie's nest in April 2008 but was quickly kicked out when Logie got back from Guinea Bissau. I was fascinated to see what she would do next.

As a five-year-old local bird, with a unique colour ring, Morven spent the early part of the summer visiting osprey nesting places in the north of Scotland, but on 9th July I live-caught her and fitted a transmitter when she was near the nest belonging to Beatrice, another of the Forres clan. We were soon getting great insights into how this osprey was living her life.

Instead of going south in late August, she flew north to the Caithness trout lochs, not far north of the distinctive mountain named Morven, from which she got her name. It's an obvious landmark, visible across the Moray Firth from where I live near Forres. She was observed there by my old friend Stan Laybourne before she migrated south, her winter quarters proving to be on the coast of Mauritania.

Returning to Scotland the following year, perseverance paid off. Logie had disappeared in September 2008 on her autumn migration, so Morven bred with Logie's old mate, Talisman, and reared one young. Morven's annual migration pattern was then established; after breeding she flew north each year to Caithness for a few weeks' trout fishing, before migrating south to the Mauritanian coast. On the spring migration north, she would stop off for a short break on the Villaviciosa estuary in northern

Spain, before undertaking the last leg to Moray. In 2011 she bred again at the same nest, but with a new male, yellow HA, and reared three young. They reared another chick in 2012 and three more in 2013. The following year, though, Morven's mate was killed by a new male before the newcomer and Morven were kicked out by a younger pair and she moved to an unused nest some miles away.

Morven was by then too late to breed in 2014, but she and her new mate reared two young in 2015 and one more in 2016. In March 2017, she was live-trapped at an artificial osprey nest on the Villaviciosa estuary by osprey biologist Doriana Pando, and the defunct transmitter was removed.

Some ospreys were very delayed by bad weather in 2017, but not Morven, who gave up waiting for her mate and moved to join an old male at another nest in the Forres area. There she reared three young. In 2018, she was at the Spanish estuary on 20th March and returned to incubate eggs, but the nesting attempt failed, possibly due to pine martens. This also happened in 2019 and 2020, but in both springs the pair moved on after a couple of days and bred in an unknown nest. Morven was also seen in March 2020 at her usual stopover on the estuary in northern Spain. In May 2021, I found her breeding at a different nest with a new mate.

Unknowingly, Morven has contributed much to osprey conservation. She has nested in four different eyries with five different mates, which is unusual for ospreys. Some of her young were translocated to the Basque reintroduction project and one was sent in 2015 to start the Swiss project. We also satellite-tagged her single young in 2012 and named him Stan, in memory of my great birding friend who had first seen Morven in Caithness, and who had died. Sadly, we lost contact with the young osprey Stan at the Cape Verde islands, after he had made an incredible nine-day, 5,000-kilometre migration over the Atlantic Ocean via the Canary Islands.

Importantly, in 2017, one of Morven's young – blue colour ring LS7 – was translocated to the Poole Harbour site. LS7 was a young male, the first to fly from the hacking cages at Poole Harbour when we started the latest reintroduction project in partnership with Birds of Poole Harbour. He was a winner: attacked by a peregrine on his first flight at 5.45am on 31st July 2017, he soon settled down to feed up from fresh fish supplied by the project team. He was the first to leave on migration on 25th August and his post-fledging period of twenty-five days was the equal shortest of the eight young that year. On 22nd January 2018 he was seen and identified on the Île des Oiseaux ('island of birds') in Senegal by Adam Lene, a ranger in the Sine-Saloum National Park. Both my colleague Tim Mackrill and I have visited this fantastic sandy island off the mangrove swamps; it's an osprey mecca.

It is always a long two-year's wait to see which ospreys have survived their first migrations and extended stays in West Africa and then return to the UK. Of the Poole Harbour releases, LS7 was our first return as a two-year-old, seen and identified by Paul Morton on 12th June. Almost immediately LS7 met the well-known female, blue CJ7, which had fledged from a nest at Rutland Water in 2015. She has been a regular at Poole Harbour and in spring built up nests around the harbour and kept an eye out for a mate. Too late to breed in 2019, their activity together boded well for the future.

That July, the next group of eleven young Scottish ospreys were taken to the new Poole Harbour hacking cages, and both LS7 and CJ7 took an interest in the new cohort of young ospreys. This is very important behaviour as it mimics being in an osprey breeding area. All of them were released between 3rd and 5th August and all except one – which had been predated by a fox on 2nd September, just days before leaving – set off for Africa.

In 2020, the female CJ7 was back at her favourite nest and waited in vain for LS7 or another young male; she even laid infertile eggs. Unfortunately, it was the poorest spring migration for ospreys I have ever known. A large area of persistent high pressure over Britain gave us beautiful sunny weather throughout April, but that weather system creates strong easterly winds and often cloudy, wet conditions in Iberia, meaning that migrating ospreys can get swept out into the Atlantic Ocean and die, or be seriously delayed. In Scotland, more adults than in any previous season failed to return and, very disappointingly, blue LS7 did not reappear. Did he die or was he simply so exhausted that he abandoned his flight north? At the time of writing, we do not know.

These recovery projects often rely on small numbers of winners, ospreys which have made it through their first years, learning the migration routes and wintering sites, and have survived the associated dangers of bad weather and predators. Projects are always unpredictable: the pandemic meant that we were unable to translocate more young in 2020. We are hopeful, though, that the first pair from the Poole Harbour project will breed in 2021, starting a restored breeding population in the south coast estuaries. Then we can say that the mullet hawk is back.

The paradox of Pallas's sandgrouse

In 1888, an amazing ornithological event happened just ten miles from where I now live. It was completely unexpected, and it would be incredibly surprising if it should ever happen again there.

A Pallas's sandgrouse nested in the sand desert of Culbin, an appropriate place because the species is a bird of the great sand deserts of Mongolia and northern China. Culbin at that time was a wild and transient series of shifting sand dunes stretching westwards for ten miles from the mouth of the River Findhorn in Moray along the south shore of the Moray Firth to the town of Nairn. The dunes were so mobile that the moving sands in their time had completely overwhelmed a village, a manor house and the fertile farmland around it.

In the early part of the 20th century, the fledgling Forestry Commission started to plant a major conifer forest to bind the blowing sand, creating the 3,000-hectare Culbin Forest, now a regular birding haunt of mine. I've often thought about the sandgrouse and wondered where exactly the nest and young had been. There'll be no return for it, now that the landscape has been transformed. It is, though, still possible to climb the great dunes of sands within a sylvan setting and in one lovely area marvel at a lichen-covered plain of pebbles, dotted with 'bonsai' Scots pines that have always struggled to grow between the pure, rounded stones.

The Pallas's sandgrouse is an interesting and special bird; part of its scientific name – *paradoxus* – gives us a clue to its nature. The first part of its name refers to the German explorer and naturalist Peter Simon Pallas (1741–1811), who killed and collected some specimens on one of his expeditions into the Russian Asian deserts, under the patronage of Empress Catherine II of Russia. There are a dozen species of sandgrouse in the world, medium-sized birds resembling a mix between a partridge, a pigeon and a plover, often with a long tail. They live and breed in desert conditions and have a very special adaptation for such dry climates. In the mornings and evenings, they gather in flocks and fly to fresh water, often many miles away. There they drink and then waddle into the water to soak the feathers of their breast and underparts to store water, the plumage allegedly more efficient than a sponge. When they return to the breeding site, the young can snuggle under the adults' bodies and drink moisture, which is a very clever adaption for a species that makes its home in deserts.

I saw my first Pallas's sandgrouse 7,000 kilometres east of Culbin, in the Gobi Desert of Mongolia. In June 1980 I was leading a birding tour to Siberia and Mongolia for my friend Mark Beaman. It was an amazing journey with fantastic birding in places that I had often dreamt of visiting. On 13th June we flew from Ulaanbaatar airport to the Gobi Desert Camp – an incredible 'holiday camp' destination for Communist-bloc Europeans in the days of restricted travel, where they could lie in the sun and drink local beer. From there, a four-wheel-drive bus took us out into the desert to our campsite near a lake called Ulaan Nuur. In the evening a couple of flocks of sandgrouse flew over where we were camping, near big reed beds, but it was the next day that I really got to know the bird.

We were up for a 5am birding walk towards the lake, and the first entry in my field notebook for that day is that Pallas's sandgrouse were calling and flying everywhere. They were on their early-morning visit to drink and soak up water in the lake; I noted their buff plumage and black bellies. There was a tremendous sunrise across the Mongolian desert with clear, brilliant skies; some distance from us came the mumbling of a herd of camels tethered around the herders' yurts. We saw Kentish plovers, a redshank, paddyfield warblers, Blyth's pipits and citrine wagtails. It was the sandgrouse that were outstanding, though: they were everywhere, flying in fast flocks to and from the lake with their delightful chirruping flight calls, 'prrrp – prrrp'. We reckoned there were at least 500, with the stunning outline of the distant Gobi-Altai mountains forming the southern backdrop to the scurrying flocks. What a bird and what a place – nesting in Culbin sands must have been a bit of a let-down.

The next day, we saw at least 200 on our birding tour, while two days later, on a pre-breakfast walk in the desert near the Gobi Desert Camp, we saw a dozen. Ten years later, I visited Mongolia and the Gobi Desert again, travelling with three friends on a recce for an Operation Raleigh expedition. On 11th September 1990, we flew in two aged Antonov aircraft from Hovd, in the furthest west region of Mongolia, and landed 200 kilometres to the south at the gravel runway at Bulgan, just north of the Chinese border. It was 9.20 on a clear cool morning at the desert oasis and I saw sixteen Pallas's sandgrouse (and six ravens) flying south over the airstrip, as the plane took off in a cloud of dust and we drove into town. Those were the only ones I saw in three weeks of an autumn visit.

In the past, this species was subject to great irruptions, and in May 1863 and May 1888 spectacular invasions reached Western Europe, including the British Isles. In the latter year, two clutches of eggs were found near Beverley in Yorkshire, while pairs bred in two places in coastal Moray. A nest and eggs were found in June 1888 and at least one brood of young was recorded in August 1889. The invasion was a major ornithological event and is well documented in the history books, with landowners at Culbin Sands and Lossiemouth instructing their gamekeepers to protect the birds. It is without doubt one of the outstandingly strange events in the ornithological history books and it is still possible, when you walk over the dunes at Culbin, to imagine the excitement at what had happened 130 years before. A smaller invasion happened in 1908 but since then the bird has been a very rare vagrant, with the last on Shetland in May 1990.

When I was in Mongolia in 1980, we were also fortunate to see a juvenile Pallas's sea eagle on 14th June. It was feeding at the remains of a dead camel, much to the consternation of our Mongolian guide, Pulcher, from the state travel agency, Zuulchin. Pulcher did not want us to photograph dead animals, as he was sure we had none in the west. We could not have cared less about the carcass: we just wanted photos of the eagle, the only one we recorded. We knew that Pallas's cat also lived in the area but did not see one.

In retrospect, it seems strange that these three iconic species in the Gobi should carry the name of a long-dead German zoologist, whose name is also attached to ten other animal species. That, though, is the history of European scientific discovery. The locals had known the sandgrouse for centuries, even millennia, for it was – and is – such a distinctive bird within their lives as desert herders. They, like the bird, knew the lakes where fresh water was to be found. Marco Polo visited Asia in the late 13th century and used the name *bargherlac* to describe the bird that was undoubtedly what we now call the Pallas's sandgrouse. I was recently reading about the North American trend to look critically at the naming of birds, and that the McCown's longspur has recently been renamed the thick-billed longspur, Mr McCown's actions in history no longer being acceptable to us. Maybe it's time that *paradoxus* be renamed the Gobi sandgrouse, locating it firmly where it has always properly belonged.

Wilding rewilding

It's 7th March, and I set off this morning to make my usual circuit of the local forest, a long, lone walk being the very best way, I find, for me to wrestle my thoughts into order. Walking helps me with assembling my ideas about nature and considering what direction we should take with a big-scale restoration of our planet. I enjoyed hearing the newly returned robins and chaffinches singing in the thickets when I got to what our family will always call the Gruffalo Tree, a nickname borrowed from a neighbour's boy for a huge Douglas fir by the forest gate. Further on, in the more mature trees, I heard siskins and crossbills, but it was a dreich morning, with clouds so low that they wet me without raining.

I was thinking about where we need to head as more and more rewilded land is given to nature recovery. We will have to think of what else is required: not just rewilding, but the subsequent stages of ecological restoration. What we accepted as normal in the past may become one of the big obstacles to taking the vision further.

I know this forest well and nowadays there are no apex predators, because wolf, lynx and brown bear are all long gone. The middle-guild predators – badger, fox, pine marten and otter – are now top of the pile and are often in high numbers because they have no pressure from above. This cascades down as extra predation on the remaining species; hole-nesting birds like tits, for example, find it increasingly difficult to fledge their young successfully in dead trees when plentiful martens examine every potential nest cavity. Badgers replicate that with ground-nesting birds, and otters with nesting waterfowl.

We have to try to recreate the impact of the trophic chains of old. Until the apex predators are restored, *we* have to be the apex predator, not in the ways of the past when the human aim was often extermination, but in a holistic, wildlife management way that mimics and replicates natural processes. That will require reductions in the middle-guild predators to try to balance ecological restoration. This will be a difficult concept for many to accept.

Easier to take on board may be a reappraisal of how we control deer populations. In future – on nature reserves, scientific sites and rewilding areas – we should shoot deer with copper rather than lead ammunition, and we should not be removing the carcasses. We should also do what apex predators do when they have killed a deer, have a really good feed (in our case, remove the saddle and haunches) but leave all the remainder for scavenging meat-eating birds, mammals and invertebrates. Additionally, shooting should be random throughout the whole range and across the annual cycle, again mirroring natural predation.

We also need, in the long term, to think about the redundancy of some present wildlife management activities. I've always thought of nest boxes for birds, bats and insects as a bit like sticking plasters; we have to have them because we've drastically reduced woodland for centuries, cut down all the dead trees for firewood and tidied up the woods so that natural holes are really scarce. But when fifty per cent of the land has been rewilded for decades, there will be enough natural nesting holes for birds, and nest boxes will become a thing of the past. The same thinking should be applied to feeding birds with non-native food such as peanuts and fat balls. I think that such feeding skews the avian fauna, selecting certain species that are capable of making the switch from natural foods in the forest to relying on bird feeders. Once we rewild the habitats in a big way, we will need to rewild the species.

This worry often comes to the surface of my mind when I see whooper swans, those splendid, beautiful waterfowl that come south from Iceland to winter with us, sailing across our landscape with their wonderful trumpeting calls. During winters in the 1960s and 1970s I'd see families and small groups scattered on lochs and marshes throughout the Scottish Highlands, with a larger wintering flock on the Insh Marshes. They were all eating natural plant material and seeds. Large-scale feeding with maize and cereals then started up at nature reserves, allowing visitors the spectacle of large flocks close up. Those birds that had scraped a reasonable living in natural places found themselves at a disadvantage compared to the 'fed' ones and soon joined the queue. Now I no longer see swan families at my favourite lochs of yesteryear, where once I could watch them upending to eat water plants on the sandy bottom. To me, that's a loss of naturalness, but also – in an era of human pandemic – it is pertinent to remind ourselves that artificially feeding large numbers of wild birds in concentrated areas will be a risky habit to be in when the next avian disease comes along. These birds, too, need rewilding.

So as we win the argument about devoting much larger areas of the Earth's surface to nature and ecological functions, we also have to learn how to encourage nature to go back to nature and stop relying on us to put out food on bird tables or build nest boxes. It has to be done, and it's not impossible. Along my track this morning I saw recent work by the Forestry Commission: a big stand of lodgepole pine and larch had been harvested and all the dead trees left standing. What a gain for nature. That would never have happened in state forests thirty years ago, when tidiness was sacrosanct. Now, when trees are replanted or regenerate there, raptors can perch on the tall stumps by day and owls by night, hunting rodents that may have damaged young trees. Even our view of the mechanically flailed edges of the forest track needs assessing in a rewilding way: it may look a mess when the flail has been past, but its effect is no different from the actions of long-lost large herbivores. Ecological restoration or rewilding requires a recognition of multiple processes over time, many of which require changes within our own minds and prejudices.

The bearded vulture, a rewilding icon

It's summer 2020 and I've just read my latest copy of *British Birds*, in which it is reported that a bearded vulture, recently seen in the Peak District, might be repatriated. It says that any intervention would be a last resort, but that the bird would be returned safely to its 'home reintroduction area'. It's neither ringed nor radio-tagged, nor marked in any way, so is not a freshly released bird from one of the reintroduction projects in the Alps, the Massif Central or Andalusia. Where, then, in fact, is 'home'? The main question seems to be about its authenticity as a wild bird, as with the one that visited the UK in May 2016. That matters if you want to count it on your British life list, but the question mark over the bird's origins hasn't discouraged the hundreds of birders that have ventured into the hills and enjoyed seeing it.

But why, if it is a wild bird, should it be repatriated? Such a long-distance wanderer, if it is in good condition, could find its own way back to wherever it came from, provided it has found enough food and decided it did not wish to stay. So why should there not be enough food, even though it follows other scavengers, such as buzzards and ravens, to the remains of a few dead sheep? And if there is enough food, why not leave it where it is, in case another bearded vulture turns up next May? Vultures might then breed in Britain – maybe they have before? In fact, instead of talking of repatriation, why not bring in some other vultures from mainland Europe to join it? At some stage, the very successful bearded vulture projects will mean that the present range will become full and young ones will have to find new breeding places. What a marvellous prospect that is.

Worldwide, vultures have suffered hard times. In India and Pakistan, the common three vulture species crashed from a population of millions to 20,000. The cause was poisoning through ingesting the veterinary drug diclofenac, commonly used there to treat cattle. Research and conservation have stemmed some, but not all, of that decline. Nearer home, in southern Europe, vultures suffered from the EU regulations of the 1970s requiring the removal of dead farm animals from open land. Fortunately, sense prevailed and derogations allowed for vulture feeding places, or 'restaurants', to be established. The vultures bounced back there, but here in Britain we don't even see an excessively tidy countryside as a problem.

At the heart of that problem lies the fact that modern humans have broken the ancient food chains whereby large scavengers cleaned up the dead in nature. Nowadays, by law, apart from in exceptional circumstances, farmed livestock that die in the open have to be collected and removed, while the large predators like wolf, that killed wild deer and left as much as they ate, are long gone. Life for carrion eaters – from vultures to burying beetles – has been made nearly impossible. In my book *Cottongrass Summer*, I wrote of the appalling impacts of removing biomass and bones from the environment.

As a start, no carcasses should be removed from nature reserves or designated sites. Deer hunters must use copper bullets to prevent lead poisoning. And the establishment of raptor feeding places should be extended beyond the successful red kite locations that have been so appreciated by birders. I've recommended that several carrion 'restaurants' be set up on the south coast to attract white-tailed eagles, both the newly reintroduced ones and the increasing numbers of wintering birds from the mainland. It would be a boon for nature to have specially fenced enclosures of a couple of acres, to exclude dogs and foxes, in which local farmers could leave dead livestock. It would start another process in essential rewilding.

In fact, a few enterprising farmers could set up eco-businesses, allowing birders and photographers, in hides, to enjoy close-up spectacles of sea eagles, buzzards, ravens and even white storks feasting on carrion. It works in Spain and Portugal. Vultures cruising the coasts of France might then see the thermalling carrion eaters and cross the English Channel to investigate. It's not too far, for vultures regularly fly across the Straits of Gibraltar, while in November 2008 over a hundred griffon vultures made a much greater over-sea flight from the Spanish mainland to the Balearic Islands, some staying to breed on Majorca. The Peak District bearded vulture is an icon of that rewilding future so, for goodness' sake, why not start a vulture feeding station immediately? It is a national park and this should be a priority. To allow it to starve would be irresponsible.

*

I later heard the excellent news that the bearded vulture survived for nearly three months in the Peak District, before making a side trip to the Fens in late September. There, in its search for carrion, it was at times at risk beside busy roads. It was then observed on 15th October 2020 flying out over Beachy Head on the Sussex coast and on over the English Channel. That's not the end of the story, though, for two discarded feathers had been collected from a roost site in the Peak District. The Vulture Conservation Foundation sent them for DNA profiling and was able to identify the individual – how cool is that? The vulture (a female) had been reared as a wild nestling in 2019 in the Haute-Savoie region of the French Alps. Not only that: its male parent was a wild-fledged young from the same region and its mother had been reared at La Garenne Zoo in Switzerland in 2006 and released that autumn in the South Tyrol in Italy. What an amazing end to the story of this bearded vulture's visit to England.

I still think there should be dedicated vulture or eagle carrion restaurants operating in the national parks. Although my good friend Derek Gow has now set up a feeding table for raptors in North Devon and our project team keeps one active at the sea eagle release site on the Isle of Wight, we really need more vulture feeding stations in England. Please don't let us wait for the next vulture to come along; in fact, as I finish this essay, an adult bearded vulture has been seen in Suffolk. I really think that, with a little help from us, they could even breed successfully in England one day.

Chalk and cheese conservation

Throughout my life, I've been struck by the fact that we treat wildlife species in the sea quite differently from those on land. In my view, the inequality of species conservation between the terrestrial and marine environments is no longer tenable. I think it's time that we had similar legislation to cover both, protecting all species and habitats in the seas while allowing productive use of our waters in a sustainable manner. As a society, we also need to look afresh at the areas sustainably fished, the areas protected from fishing and who is – and who should be – permitted to fish.

Here is a fictitious but perfectly believable example of our divergent thinking. A foreign buyer is looking for a ready supply of small bats to sell in his country, where there is a market for them as a foodstuff: 'I can pay $50 each for them. I have been told that bats are common in the UK and that they can be a nuisance in roof spaces. We would like to harvest them and export them as a delicacy.' There would be a thunderous 'No!' in response. 'Bats are specially protected and what you suggest is illegal!' we would say. In another scenario, a buyer says he has a foreign client searching for exciting new varieties of very small shellfish and sea anemones; these are an exceptional delicacy in his country. The reply could quite easily be: 'Well, we don't harvest them at present, but those species are not protected under our legislation and they are not subject to quota regulations, so we can put you in contact with potential suppliers.' It could be good business for our fishermen, it could boost our export earnings, but there would almost certainly be no checks on stocks or sustainability. That really is chalk and cheese conservation.

I'm sure that's happened many times to marine species. When I think back to my early days in Shetland in the 1960s, the islanders were fishing for lobsters that were sent for live export. It was a good earner for crofter fishermen. They also caught brown crabs and, occasionally, squat lobsters, both of which in those days were thrown back into the sea, with a few of the larger ones given to locals like us to eat. Then, as conditions for export got better, brown crabs were fished and sent to market with the lobsters, then the squat lobsters joined them, along with velvet crabs in the 1980s, followed by an increasing variety of marine species. More recently, the trade in brown crab boomed as China imported ever more, until suddenly imports were banned because of cadmium levels in the brown meat. There's an amazingly good markets for dog whelks, too. I've known them all my life and never considered them a food item. How wrong I was: the Koreans love them, so our expensive whelks take the long flight east.

I remember as a child cooking winkles and taking a needle to tease them out and eat them. I knew they were gathered around the shores and sold. I also remember my older daughter going with classmates on a survival weekend in north-west Sutherland and finding winkles a lifesaver, given that the group had not been allowed to bring food with them and had to forage where they camped on the shore. Take these tiny examples and multiply them on a national scale, though, and the harvesting of marine food becomes irrational and unstrategic, following a boom-and-bust pattern, which makes it very difficult to safeguard the wise use of valuable species.

At the moment, anything under the waves is pretty much ripe for exploitation, while on land there are clear guidelines on the protection of species and on conservation and sustainable use. It's true that the protection of endangered species at sea – whales and dolphins, for example, and some special fish, rare marine organisms and special habitats – is increasing. Some people might argue that the marine protection areas are adequate for the needs of marine ecosystems. But they are not: most of them are still fished with damaging gear. Fishermen would say that sensitive species and locations can be protected when needed, but many species do not even have quotas. The only way a problem with a species is recognised as serious is when so few remain that it's no longer worth fishing for them. In such a crucial period for saving the planet from biodiversity collapse, we can no longer afford to think this way.

The next step should be to review the methods of fishing for the fish we eat. The public who eat fish will want the fishing industry to be increasingly sustainable and much less damaging to the marine environment, or they will stop buying it. Maybe fish should be more expensive to reflect the cost to our seas? There have been attempts to make fishing activity at sea greener. Some fisheries are easier than others: langoustines, for example, can be caught in creels instead of via bottom trawling, allowing small ones to survive and the best to be in perfect condition. The fishermen can select those of the correct size for human consumption and put the rest back into the water. Dredging for scallops and clams causes too much damage to non-target species and habitats, whereas divers can harvest them without harming their surroundings. Some of us can remember the Cod War, the dispute between the UK and Iceland over fishing rights. Once Iceland had control of their waters, they abandoned dragging fish up in trawls and turned to fishing with long lines and hooks, considerably increasing the quality of each fish and its by-products. The present drastic levels of by-catch of protected and rare fish must be eliminated, or at least reduced, by seeking new methods of catching. Major change is needed.

Some will say that change is not possible, but just think of how Scottish and British law over the sea has shifted over the decades. The original limit to territorial waters of three nautical miles was related to cannon-shot range and the distance from which one could identify boats, whether friend or foe. This merged into an international limit of three miles in 1889. In 1964 the government extended this to twelve nautical miles from the UK mainland or any island. Later discussions about the territorial shelf resulted in a 200-kilometre fishery limit in 1978, which led to exclusive economic zones, exclusive use for energy developments and, in 1996, to the protection and preservation of the marine environment. This last measure is important and should be the guiding legislation for nature at sea.

Fishing and resource conservation has started to examine the principle of designating protected fishing in enclosed bays and sea lochs. This should go further and control the methods of fishing, excluding damaging ones in certain areas, for example in the Moray Firth, part of which is a designated Special Conservation Area. Bottom trawling should be banned but selective fisheries could be permitted in zones, with fishing effort based on careful selection of species and sustainability.

That brings us to who will be the fishermen of the future. Originally it was principally those people around the coast who could get to the fishing grounds safely and efficiently in open boats from their own harbours. As oars and sails were replaced by engines, boats got bigger and, with larger and more effective trawlers, fish stocks declined. Fishermen ranged further and further from home, and over-fishing and damage to the seabed was no longer on their own doorstep.

For Scotland to have a long term, truly sustainable future in fishing, a major overhaul is required. Some basic principles might be that we fish sustainably in our own waters, that we have exclusive use of our own seas and that we don't fish in other countries' waters. In this way, coastal communities could truly protect their livelihoods, and fish would be there for their grandchildren. The government needs to take back control of all quotas. Quotas were not meant to belong solely to individuals and companies, some of whom may not reside in the UK. The fish are a resource for Scotland as a nation but they are also a crucial part of the Earth's marine environment. Their wise use should be divided equitably to the benefit of coastal fishing communities. That will be a big ask but unless something is done, the future sustainability of fish stocks is simply not possible. More importantly, the actual growing of the stock to original population levels should be a guiding principle – for example, twenty per cent of a higher restored stock would be better than forty per cent of the present stock levels.

The other pressing need for marine life is that protected areas must be designated as 'No fishing' and 'No damaging use' whatsoever. They must be unique zones for regeneration and should protect fifty per cent of our marine environment. They would require firm policing but if technological innovation allows farmers to geo-fence cattle on grazings with no physical fences, why should we not be able to geo-fence trawlers out of protected areas? It is essential that we have a fair and well-planned network of protected no-fished areas adjacent to fished areas throughout our exclusive-use seas. Fish and marine organisms in the protected areas would increase and spread out into fisheries zones. This would give security to fishermen to make their living and bring ashore a range of fish and shellfish and, in future, other harvests for human consumption, such as seaweeds. It must result in fish being more valued and used optimally, which in turn would give a better living to coastal communities.

The present use of the seas does not stand up to scrutiny and is no longer the way to go forward. It's the duty of governments to sort out these problems.

Rewilding offshore islands

It's fifty years since I mist-netted and ringed storm petrels on Fair Isle, but I can still recall their purring call, the soft plumage and – above all – their distinctive, musky scent. It was magical, the way that scent would cling to the mist-net bag, to be released a year or so later when it was time to go ringing again. There was no doubt that scent was important to those birds.

And so I was interested to read a paper on shearwaters by Tim Guilford, published in the journal *British Birds*. I was fascinated by his team's experiments, trying to understand the olfactory abilities of shearwaters for navigation and homing. I wrote to the author because I've always believed that the smell of shearwaters and petrels was also important to them for finding their homes and nest burrows in their ancestral woodland habitats.

Originally, before the arrival of humans and grazing livestock, offshore islands would have been wooded. Petrels and shearwaters would therefore have lived on islands covered in trees and long vegetation. When they come ashore at night, the birds are ungainly, their legs weak and little adapted for walking – they are, after all, the ultimate seabirds. It's probable that their olfactory abilities helped to guide them to their own nesting burrows in amongst the woodlands. Now, people know them as living on bare islands – the overgrazed mountains of Rum in the Inner Hebrides, home to the biggest colony of Manx shearwaters in the world, or the Leach's petrel colony on the sheep-grazed boulder slope of Carn Mor on St Kilda, but these are human-degraded landscapes. In some islands in the world, in Japan, Australia and North America, shearwaters and petrels still come ashore at night to breed as a woodland species in undamaged habitat.

Millennia ago, as the first humans journeyed by boat to the off-shore islands, they brought livestock – including goats and sheep – and fire, to destroy the woodland and scrub to create grazing for their stock. This meant that their sheep and goats were safe from mainland predators like wolves. In Scotland, all the offshore islands from Shetland south to the Uists, and even out to St Kilda, were dramatically altered by humans and their livestock. The petrels and shearwaters had to make do with an altered landscape that makes them more easily predated. Large numbers of the rare Leach's petrels of St Kilda, for example, have become night-time prey for great skuas.

In recent decades, a really encouraging recovery of breeding seabirds has occurred as rat eradication programmes have been carried out on our offshore islands. I believe that the next step is to ecologically restore the offshore islands by regenerating and reinstating the original tree species, such as willows, birch, rowan and hazel. It should be easier than trapping rats, for it simply requires the removal of the introduced grazers, such as Soay sheep on Hirta and blackface sheep on Boreray, red deer and goats on Rum. There are many small islands from which sheep should be removed and where woodland restoration should be started. If the unnatural, bare slopes of Carn Mor on St Kilda were re-wooded, the Leach's petrels would be safer from skuas and large gulls, while woodland scrub regeneration on the Flannans and North Rona would also benefit them. Just imagine the eerie calling of Manx shearwaters on Rum echoing from within a deciduous scrub forest.

We as a species have degraded the offshore islands throughout the British Isles, along with other amazing seabird islands throughout the oceans of the world. Let's start a bold programme to rewild and rewood the offshore islands, to complement and build on the excellent work we have already done in exterminating rats.

Autumn

Landmarks of a year

During the first year of the pandemic, we were all forced to slow down and spend more time in our own localities. For many people, it offered an unexpected chance to reconnect with nature. We had time to dawdle in the park, sit with our children on the riverbank and – for those fortunate enough to have a garden – appreciate the flowers, notice the butterflies passing through or look up to see what's flying overhead, which for once was not sharing its airspace with planes criss-crossing the globe. Craning our necks would more likely have shown us house martins flying to nests under the eaves, ribbons of gulls heading to and from a wetland roost or even – for a lucky few – a huge sea eagle high overhead. And although we had no idea of it at the outset, we had the chance to observe nature in all the seasons, as spring changed to summer and then to autumn, offering a release from lockdown before the chill of the 'stay at home' message which winter brought once more.

In a terrible time for humans – provoked, ironically enough, by a naturally occurring virus – nature offered us joy and the potential of a sense of wellbeing. Despite everything, nature maintained its annual rhythms and continued to weave its fabric of perpetuity. That sense of continuity always gives me reassurance, however bad the news.

For me, the start of the year is closely associated with the dark nights of northern Scotland: the incredible display of stars, the shimmering of the aurora and the brilliance of the full moon lighting up the landscape. The hooting of a tawny owl sounds so much louder on cold, clear nights and, on some mornings, I wake to shimmering hoar frost on the birch trees.

When winter wanes and spring is on the horizon, I am keen to see the signs of its arrival. If I venture onto the mosses, I search for the inconspicuous, greyish spikes of cottongrass pushing up towards the sun. When I find the first, I just cannot resist drawing it out and marvelling at the green growth below: then I know that life is returning. In the blustery spring squalls, the branches rattling, I'll hear the distant, wild song of a mistle thrush, a precursor to us here in the north of the real sign of spring: not the swallow or cuckoo, but the pied wagtail – or, as I call it, the 'polly dishwasher', in a throwback to my youth in Hampshire. Its march across the roof tiles is as sure a sign of new life as the big patch of butterbur on one of my regular walking routes. It grows under a grove of old trees, edged round by wild garlic; the butterbur bearing flowers before its leaves, the garlic showing its rich green leaves before it blooms.

April is joyous, the first of a run of my three favourite months of the year. The ospreys are back, and I have a shiver of recognition when I look at the first with my telescope, seeing that wild yellow eye observing me. The greenness of the fresh leaves of birch and larch always stirs me, and on the moors I love to hear the bubbling of a curlew on its home patch. In the garden, it's the first tortoiseshell butterfly of the spring that beckons me; I see the queen wasps in the gooseberry flowers, then everything quickens. Warblers' song surrounds me, sand martins buzz in the sand pit and, later, the drift of yellow pollen from the ancient Scots pines paints the dark waters of the loch.

Summer brings the harvests – black juicy cherries in the gean tree, irresistible to me. It's odd that the ends of natural lives are less noted than the spring beginnings, but it's impossible to miss the 'wink-wink' calls of migrating pink-footed geese from Iceland. Peering upwards to the ever-changing patterns of the skeins, I note how very high they are, for they have made the great crossing of the ocean and are now 'seatbelts fastened' for the southward glide to Perthshire. Soon the red squirrels will dash past our windows to collect nuts from the hazel trees and when I go to the mountains to hear the stags or watch for salmon, the yellow and red leaves of autumn aspens will be stunning. The fieldfares and redwings arrive en masse and gorge on ripe, red rowan berries before my least-liked month, November, drifts us into the freezing beauty of our northern winter.

Whatever change a single year might bring, the natural cycle has always kept me steady. Nature guided me through the pandemic year, as it has every year; it has always given me a star by which to steer.

The altruism of diligent creatures

The jays are flying high again because it's October. For the rest of the year they rather skulk around the woods, only their raucous calls letting us know that they are there. Now, though, the oak trees are full of ripe acorns and the birds are busy harvesting.

Their noisy, chattering calls and their love of acorns both feature in the jay's scientific name, *Garrulus glandarius*. Their harvest begins in September and reaches a peak in mid-October, when the acorns are ripe and at their best. By then, the jays may be carrying out six caching flights an hour from dawn to dusk. By mid-November, the acorn harvest will be over for the year. Each jay may collect and carry 3,000 or more acorns in an autumn, choosing the biggest and best and eating only those that have already been nibbled by bugs. When caching, a jay will stuff four or five acorns into its gullet, get the last one gripped in its bill, leave the trees and fly high across the countryside instead of low into woods.

I saw them yesterday morning when I was out for a walk. The jays were taking the acorns about three-quarters of a mile – although they can easily fly twice that distance – to a scraggy area of small trees and grassland to bury their future food supplies. But why do they fly so high? It cannot be that they want to know where they're going, so I wonder if it's to avoid predators while they are carrying their precious cargo. Jays feature regularly in the diet of goshawks living in the forests.

The jays hide the acorns in disturbed soil, leaf mould, grassland and places with cover, which is exactly where young oak trees grow best. In closed woodland, the oak saplings can be out-competed by other tree species. Growing in the open, such as within brambles, they get an early break from being browsed down by deer while they also get a chance to develop their broad, branching structure. Most of the acorns are eaten later by the jays, of course, for they remember where their caches are. Some will be missed, though; and individual jays may die – for example, killed by a goshawk; and other acorns will be eaten by rodents. But enough will remain undiscovered. This allows oak trees to grow in new places and oak woodland to be extended. Later, in May and June, jays will sometimes notice the fresh greenness of the seedling oaks and pull them up to eat the fresh cotyledons, but often the tree will survive.

Jays only reached the north of Scotland forty years or so ago and oaks and, in a few places, sweet chestnut seedlings, reaching for the sky away from mother trees, are very clear pointers as to where the birds have moved acorns. As they fly day by day through the acorn season, the jays work hard in what really is a true act of altruism. The symbiotic relationship of jays planting acorns ensures that there will be more oak trees in the future, but those birds, as individuals, are not going to benefit. The oaks and jays of the future will, though, and so will an incredible number of species that benefit from the growth of oak trees. Even we will benefit, in many ways, including in the ability of oak trees to take in carbon and release oxygen via photosynthesis.

As the jays start their autumn harvest, the red squirrels are finishing theirs. They have been busy through September, gathering hazelnuts from the grooves of hazel trees that grow along the bank below my house. The squirrels come from the pinewood about a hundred yards across the road, but there must be others as well, from further afield, who know that September is the month to gather hazelnuts. Some days, as I sit at my desk, I watch them scurry back and forth, round the house, across the lawn, up over my woodpile, through the lilac hedge and into the first hazel tree. I can see them clambering around in the upper branches and then, in no time at all, they return over the woodpile and across the lawn with a mouthful of hazelnuts. They usually head for the pinewood to store their haul in secret places.

On other days, though, they just potter around on the lawn, choose places that seem to have no merit, have a quick little dig, push a nut into the hole and pat the grass down quickly with their front paws in a nonchalant manner. Then on they go, onto the next. Some days they bury dozens. I never know how they find them again. I'm told they remember the most likely places and may smell the nuts, but they certainly don't find them all, because young hazel trees are always popping up in unexpected places in the garden, as well as in many places on the surrounding land. The red squirrel is such a great creator of new hazel trees. It's another example, in my view, of altruism towards future squirrels, creating hazel thickets appreciated both by wildlife and by us.

When I was young, I remember, we boys would search for really good hazel sticks to make bows or catapults, while older people in the farming districts made an annual harvest of hazel wands to season for walking sticks and handles for various farm implements. Before the middle of the last century, every crofting township or farming community had its own protected hazel wood, from which domestic stock was fenced out. Hazels were important in people's lives. One of my old farmer friends would walk each year to select and cut some suitable hazel sticks; he had two favourite places, half a mile apart. Once they were dried, and often with a sheep horn handle fitted to the top, he would present them to friends. This hazel work survives as a craft, but he was doing what his family and ancestors had been doing for decades, even centuries and more. Those favourite hazel groves of his may originally have been planted by a squirrel, in a lovely example of mammal and mankind working together.

A great day's birding

Fair Isle, between Orkney and the Shetland Isles, has been special to me since I spent my first year there as an assistant warden in 1959. The sea birds living on the great cliffs are fantastic, but an amazing variety of migrant birds also visit this tiny island, out there alone betwixt the Atlantic Ocean and the North Sea. It is a welcome landfall for migrating birds. Some days, during a big migration fall, the birding can be more exciting than anywhere else in Britain.

In autumn 1998, I was staying at the Bird Observatory for its 50th anniversary, which luckily coincided with one of those purple patches for bird migrants on the island. I arrived on Saturday 3rd October and was met at the airstrip by Helen Baker from the observatory. She had with her a spotted crake, just caught for ringing in the Vaadal trap. I left my rucksack in the observatory's van and walked straight down to Boini Mire, close to the island shop, to look for and finally find the Pallas's grasshopper warbler, which had been seen earlier. I had seen the species in Siberia, but never in Britain, so was delighted when the skulking little bird showed itself well in the long grass. Before going back to the observatory, I saw a lovely streaky Pechora pipit, also from Siberia, as well as two Richard's pipits, two rustic buntings, a short-toed lark and a bluethroat – all Fair Isle specialities. That evening, when I listened to the observatory warden recording the day's counts in the bird log, kept since 1948, it was clear that bird migrants were present in both quantity and quality on the island. It was perfect timing for the group of birders staying at the observatory.

Birders visit Fair Isle in spring and autumn in the hope of watching bird migration in action, as well as hoping to see really rare birds from Siberia or North America. The tree-less island has an advantage because many of the passerine birds usually live in woods, long vegetation or marshes, and are difficult to view on their home turf. On Fair Isle they stick out a mile when they perch on fences or try to hide in a rose bush. Sanity tells us that they are common where they come from, but to find a bird never before seen in Britain, or even in Europe, is the dream for many a keen birder. There's the challenge of identifying it, making sure that others see it before nightfall, and the memories it brings back of our own visits to far-off lands. Many springs ago I found the first ever song sparrow on this side of the Atlantic. A week later, birders arriving from a cruise ship divided into two groups: Europeans were eager to see a new bird while the Americans were amused by the fuss over a very common, nondescript sparrow. Nevertheless, that dedicated recording on Fair Isle has recently been used to understand bird behaviour in relation to climate changes and human impacts on the Earth.

Next morning, I was up before dawn and walked to the north end of the island, where I watched the sun rise over low grey clouds on the horizon from the North Light. Song thrushes, redwings and ring ouzels flying up from my path showed that most of the previous day's arrival was still present. A short sea watch at the lighthouse gave me gannet, fulmar, guillemot and razorbill flying past, over the sea. From my walk along the cliffs to Easter Lother, I saw black guillemots and eiders on the sea, with twenty-three wigeon on the loch, and the route back brought a lovely mix of birds, with a chiffchaff above the observatory being my 41st species before breakfast.

Afterwards, a walk down to the harbour produced a red-breasted merganser and I watched a freshly caught yellow-browed warbler being ringed at the observatory. The morning's walk to the south end of the island via the slopes of Vaasetter gave me eleven Lapland buntings and there were thirty-eight golden plovers and some ruffs at Barkland croft. The bluethroat was still in the Shirva croft garden and the Pechora pipit in the meadow below. The varied goose flock was made up of two greylags, two pinkfeet, nine barnacles and two bean geese. There was such a variety of species on the island that at lunchtime, back at the observatory, I thought I'd try for a hundred species in the day.

I was back down the island again to search the eastern side to Meoness. Purple sandpipers on the seaweed-covered rocks gave me my 88th species, and soon I had also seen shore lark, wryneck and rustic bunting. By the end of a tiring day's walking and a brilliant day's birding, I was just four species short of the hundred.

It would be interesting to know the best ever day's tally on the island: it probably comes close to 120, which is amazing for such a small island and part of what makes Fair Isle special. The bird log that evening gave a total of 108 species, showing that I had missed twelve. No one, including me, had found the skulking Pallas's grasshopper warbler, which was seen again the following day. Shoveler, peregrine, water rail, spotted crake, moorhen, woodcock, glaucous gull, short-eared owl, house martin, mistle thrush, whitethroat and little bunting: all had been there, had been seen by others, but not by me.

The maximum number of species seen at Fair Isle in a year is 216, in 1992. Over a hundred species have been recorded on a good number of days, but no one has personally seen a hundred species in a day on Fair Isle, or at least it's not recorded if they have – maybe I did when I was warden in the 1960s but it's too late to say that now. If only, on that day in 1998, I had not stopped on several occasions to have tea with island friends – maybe if I had commandeered the observatory van for the afternoon, I might have got those missing four species? But I suppose that's what allows me to say that I'm not a proper twitcher.

My day list for 4th October 1998: fulmar, cormorant, shag, grey heron, wigeon, mallard, teal, red-breasted merganser, eider duck, greylag, pink-footed, barnacle and bean goose, sparrowhawk, merlin, kestrel, oystercatcher, golden plover, grey plover, ringed plover, lapwing, snipe, jack snipe, curlew, redshank, spotted redshank, purple sandpiper, dunlin, curlew sandpiper, little stint, sanderling, ruff, turnstone, great black-backed gull, herring gull, common gull, black-headed gull, great skua, kittiwake, guillemot, razorbill, black guillemot, wood pigeon, rock dove, stock dove, wryneck, skylark, swallow, short-toed lark, shore lark, rock pipit, pied wagtail, yellow wagtail, Richard's pipit, rock pipit, meadow pipit, tree pipit, Pechora pipit, wren, fieldfare, blackbird, ring ouzel, redwing, song thrush, robin, bluethroat, wheatear, whinchat, redstart, reed warbler, grasshopper warbler, sedge warbler, garden warbler, blackcap, lesser whitethroat, willow warbler, chiffchaff, yellow-browed warbler, goldcrest, pied flycatcher, spotted flycatcher, dunnock, raven, hooded crow, starling, chaffinch, brambling, siskin, twite, linnet, rustic bunting, reed bunting, snow bunting, Lapland bunting, house sparrow and tree sparrow.

The Rocky Mountain goat solution

For decades now, there have been battles to control alien species such as Canada geese and grey squirrels, and most of those battles have been losing ones. Some people think they would rather see a grey squirrel come into their garden than see no squirrels at all. Given the choice, yes, they might prefer a red one, but no one has yet worked out a way of giving them that choice. It's a major dilemma, in our country and around the world.

It seems acceptable to kill alien species if they are animals the general public does not really like, such as the brown rat. Their removal by poisoning on the seabird islands from Lundy north to Canna has taken a lot of very hard work by dedicated conservationists, with really encouraging results for seabirds such as puffins, storm petrels and Manx shearwaters. Now, these birds return to breed and successfully rear young after decades of failure. The black rat, another alien brought to Britain but rare in recent decades, was defended by some mammal specialists, but its final removal from the Shiant Islands has been a boost for beleaguered seabirds. The removal of rodents that arrived with humans, then, can be a successful and much appreciated conservation exercise.

The American mink is another non-native species that has a very negative impact on birds nesting near water. Mink are a relatively modern problem, caused by their release, both intentional and unintentional, from fur farms in the second half of the 20th century, as the wearing of fur became unacceptable. With that background, it's been possible to encourage concerted efforts by many people to catch them in traps and kill them, although whether we will ever eradicate them altogether is still debatable.

Another water-loving mammal, also brought to Britain for the fur trade and now eradicated in England, was the coypu, a very large rodent from South America. These animals were a problem because they burrowed into flood banks and could therefore cause flooding, along with other kinds of damage. I remember them at Minsmere reserve in Suffolk in the early 1970s, where there were stories of impecunious young RSPB wardens eating them for dinner: they were big, provided a lot of meat and could be reasonably tasty. The removal was finally successful because a team of trappers employed in the early 1980s was told that if they eradicated them within seven years, each would receive a very handsome bonus. They killed the last one in December 1989: the cost of seven years' work was £2.5 million. The time limit was an important strategy because the offering of bounties for the eradication of other problem species has led instead to a kind of farming, the hunters killing a certain number each year, claiming the reward money but leaving enough animals to breed, creating work and an income for themselves for the following summer.

Forty years ago, I visited the Olympic National Park on the west coast of the United States, south of Seattle, a fantastically beautiful area. One day, I was up on the high mountains with a senior biologist looking at the Rocky Mountain goats, a non-native introduced from further east in the Cascades. Those big, white animals wandering among the rocks were just like any other goat I'd ever seen: they were overgrazing special plants. I was told, though, that they were the most commonly seen and distinctive mammal for visitors to the National Park, so to remove them would be highly contentious.

Contentious enough for it to have taken forty years. Some determined members of the National Park Service have now nearly got the job done. By 2020 they had captured and removed 412 of the total count of 725 a few years before; 325 had been translocated and released back into the Cascade Mountains, the native range of the species. The last ones are too difficult to catch and translocate, so will be killed out as soon as possible. It's taken major funding, a lot of dedicated work by staff, vets and volunteers, and the use of helicopters and all-terrain vehicles, demonstrating that putting nature right is a big job. I would guess that the biggest task was to persuade the general public and interested parties that this was essential conservation.

The story of the Rocky Mountain goats is a reminder of the dilemmas we face in our own country. In the Orkney Islands lives a large vole called, unsurprisingly, the Orkney vole. It is an important food for short-eared owls and hen harriers. Its presence there and nowhere else in Britain was for a long time a mystery, for how did it get there? DNA profiling has now shown that it came from mainland Europe, probably Belgium, and is thought to have arrived with early Neolithic people who settled Orkney. Did they bring it as a pet? Was it for food or fur, or was it an accidental traveller? And should it now be removed as a 'non-native'? At present there is an eradication project underway in Orkney to remove introduced stoats, so why should there be a difference between stoats and voles? Personally, I'm on the side of the Orkney vole.

My view is that the removal of ruddy ducks, a North American escapee from wildfowl collections, was necessary to protect white-headed ducks in Spain, and that hedgehogs, mistakenly taken to the Uists, should not be in the southern islands of the Outer Hebrides, eating wader eggs on the machair. I also believe that, once a decision has been made, quick action is needed. At one stage there were only a few handfuls of ring-necked parakeets roosting in trees at Twickenham, and the problems we have now could have been solved before they multiplied.

It's been demonstrated that plants can be transported very long distances by migratory wildfowl, either as seeds within their guts or stuck to their plumage. That, then, must be deemed 'natural', and this degree of the host knowing or not knowing what it is doing may have some relevance.

If you're a collector of exotic birds in the present day, have transported some illegally by plane into our country and then allowed them to be free-flying, the penalties are very high and can even involve a prison sentence. If you had done something similar in Victorian times, you would have been lauded by your peers. The length of time since the introduction of the species must be a factor, then, as must the degree of damage the alien does to native fauna and flora. Knowing the British, the degree of cuddliness must come into it as well. Eradication is easier to do if you can demonise the alien.

In conclusion, let's look at a last case, undoubtedly a difficult one but a fascinating way to test our views of the natural world. In the mid-1960s, I'd been on the island of Fetlar in the Shetland Islands with my friend Bobby Tulloch, a very well-known Shetlander and all-round naturalist. The two of us were heading home by boat; passing the small island of Hascosay, we noticed that the colony of Arctic terns was in uproar. 'The tirricks' eggs and young are being predated by a draatsie,' said Bobby – an otter was robbing the terns. The otters of Shetland are plentiful and famous, but where I lived at the time, on isolated Fair Isle, they had never occurred, for they cannot remain too long in salt water. That isolation made me think the otters had been brought to Shetland by people, just like the mice on Fair Isle, which had come from Norway. Many years later, DNA studies revealed that Shetland otters must have been brought by settlers from Norway – maybe they had a special use for otter fur. The same may well be true of the otters on Orkney and the Western Isles. Otters are predators of birds as well as fish, and Shetland should be land-mammal free, so the conclusion is obvious – but where is the bold or unwise person who would suggest the Rocky Mountain goat solution for Shetland's otters?

A record-breaking golden eagle

Way back in 1985, my diary tells me, I spent 30th June monitoring golden eagles in the north Inverness glens with my daughter Rona, who was home from Aberdeen University. We climbed to an eyrie near Cannich, which I had monitored for many years, and ringed a single eaglet – ZZ0005. I also attached two small yellow wing tags, but the eagle was never identified alive. In fact, like most ringed eagles, nothing more was heard of it – until, that is, out of the blue, I received two emails in 2018. One was from the British Trust for Ornithology (BTO) ringing scheme and the other from Gabriela Peniche, a PhD researcher on golden eagle health at the Royal (Dick) School of Veterinary Studies at Edinburgh University.

The remains of the eagle had been found near Loch Assynt in Sutherland on 10th August 2018 and were sent to the laboratory in Edinburgh. It was a male and was thought to have been dead for about six weeks. The cause of death could not be determined, but there was bruising in the skull and some suggestion of starvation. The area where it was found is 'safe' for eagles, free from illegal persecution. My view – supported by the bruising to the skull of this thirty-three-year-old bird – is that it was probably defeated and killed during a challenge by a young adult to take over a nesting site, which is a likely end for any very old breeding adult. That is how nature works for long-lived raptors.

Prior to the demise of ZZ0005, the BTO Ringing Scheme longevity data gave the longest recorded life of a ringed golden eagle as just over sixteen years: a Kielder Forest chick, ringed on 29th June 1991, had been found dead in the Scottish Borders on 7th August 2007, almost certainly due to illegal persecution. In some ways, that bird's death stimulated the South of Scotland Golden Eagle recovery project, which began in 2018. However, in Europe, the EURING (European Union for Bird Ringing) Databank has documented longevity records for two Swedish-ringed golden eagles at thirty-one years and thirty-two years, while twenty-three years is the oldest record in the United States. So ZZ0005, at thirty-three years, appears to be the world's oldest recorded ringed golden eagle. There is a record of a captive one reaching forty-six years, while very expert fieldwork on breeding pairs of golden eagles on the Isle of Skye by my old friends Kate Nellist and Ken Crane gave an annual adult survival rate of 97.5 per cent, suggesting that some adults could reach forty years of age, but with this bird we had physical evidence.

From its recovery location, it may have been the local breeding adult male living in a home range some ninety kilometres north of its natal site. I know those local eyries from my eagle fieldwork in the 1970s and 1980s. By 2010, Doug Mainland had ringed eighteen young at this location since 1990 (when ZZ0005 was five years old). On 17th June 2010, I visited the eyrie with Doug, Derek Spencer and Lorcan O'Toole, who collected one young for the Irish Golden Eagle Reintroduction Project. The other eaglet, a male, was satellite-tagged and named Suilven, and we tracked him for many years. There's just a chance that ZZ0005 may have been Suilven's male parent, establishing another of these fascinating coincidences I have seen in my lifetime working with long-lived raptors. This eaglet ranged widely when young, even briefly visiting the Isle of Skye, but as a sub-adult returned to an area just east of its natal nest. In the spring of 2015, when Suilven was five years old, the transmitter fell off (as they are meant to do) and we assume that he may still be alive and breeding in that area of Sutherland. It's lovely to think what news a couple of emails can bring, and how worthwhile that hike up the mountain with my daughter in 1985 turned out to be. It was bird ringing at its very best.

Woodcocks in trouble

One of my favourite sounds in northern Scotland, as dusk comes in, is the flight call of the woodcock. It's great fun predicting when a roding (display-flighting) male will come back round overhead and pass you again. I have always loved hearing them fly over my house, both when I lived in Strathspey and now where I am in Moray. The call is distinctive – a squeak and a grunt – uttered as the bird flies steadily about a hundred feet up, along the edges of woods and across pastures. He's looking for females and, if he sees one, will quickly fall to the ground to join it for mating. At the end of a lovely day with clear skies and no wind, after your evening meal, take a chair into the garden and sit quietly facing the last of the sun glow on the horizon. In these conditions you can hear them from several hundred metres and see them against the clear sky. It's magical but, sadly, the woodcock is in trouble.

As a child I knew woodcock in the New Forest and in some of the local woods, but my first real experience of them was in the 1960s, in a most unlikely place for this woodland bird – the cliff-encircled Fair Isle, midway between Orkney and Shetland. There I got to know them as migrants flying from Scandinavia to winter in Scotland, usually when poor weather halted their flight over the North Sea. The autumn migration in the last ten days of October and first half of November was larger than the spring one, with usually a hundred scattered over the heathery hill ground on the best days, but there was an exceptional arrival of 1,000 on 27th–28th October 1976, with the next best of 400 on 13th November 1984. In the spring there might have been a maximum of ten migrant woodcock a day, at best, except for spring peaks of 150 in 1951 and 1984. We caught and ringed small numbers every year and those later reported came from Norway, Sweden (four) and Denmark, while winter reports were from Scotland (five), Ireland (five) and England. The Fair Islanders regularly shot woodcock in autumn, and one shot on 26th October 1976 had been ringed two days earlier in Denmark.

Woodcock are most common in Scotland from November through to March, especially in the milder west, and these birds come from northern Europe. Our summer breeding birds move south-west in autumn to winter in Ireland. Some of these migrations have given us fascinating insights into their lives. In 2008 I visited a big estate on the island of Islay to give advice about the value of traditional cattle grazing in their woodlands. Woodcock shooting was one of the features of hunting on the estate, and cattle-grazing is important for this species as they feed on the plentiful worms in cattle fields and in cowpats. The following February, I returned with two tiny satellite transmitters. With the head keeper, I went out on the cattle pastures at night, armed with a powerful spotlight and a big butterfly net. We caught three woodcock, I fitted two with trackers and we waited to see what would happen.

It was not until late March that they departed on migration. One went on the northern route through Scotland and across the North Sea to Norway, while the other surprised us by flying down to Lincolnshire and across to the Netherlands and – over a period of two months – migrated north-east over Germany, the Baltic states and through Russia to its breeding location in northern Siberia, some 400 kilometres beyond the city of Archangel on Russia's north-west coast. Using Google Earth, it was possible to see that the places at which it chose to stop along the route were often close to small farms surrounded by woodland – exactly the sort of place where it could fill up on tasty invertebrates. The bird's breeding location was 4,110 kilometres from Islay.

The optimum habitat for woodcock is deciduous woodland interspersed with small grazing meadows, which provides a superb nightly supply of worms. Throughout Scandinavia, the Baltic States and Russia, this old-style agriculture has been dying out for many decades as people move to the cities, just as has happened in Scotland. These changes have been compounded in the last sixty years by expanding mechanisation and the increasing use of agricultural chemicals. Intensively worked grasslands have fewer worms and leatherjackets (cranefly larvae) than previously, while cowpats are now too toxic to be colonised by dung flies and beetles, because the cattle are treated with anthelmintics. In the past, when you walked across a field and looked at cowpats (a favourite pastime of mine), you could see where woodcock and snipe had been probing through the dung in their search for invertebrates. This was ideal food for these waders, but it's one that has been taken from them by the intensive use of chemicals to treat cattle. On top of that, the recent increase in the numbers of middle-guild mammal predators is a threat to the ground-nesting woodcock, through the predation of eggs and young.

These, then, are worrying times for woodcock, as for other breeding waders in our country. There is no doubt that life was better for all of them before the middle of the last century, stretching back into time. The tendency nowadays is to compare the numbers and breeding success of a species with twenty or forty years ago, because recent times provide the best data. When I hear someone comparing their status over such short periods, I think about the fact that the woodcock has been a species on planet Earth for between 2.6 and 5.3 million years. Across that incredible timeline, the species would have experienced tremendous ups and downs during the glacial periods, but there was plenty of time to adapt. Just imagine, before the last Ice Age, making that spring migration up into Russia and Siberia and living alongside woolly mammoths. Not only would the landscape have been different, with these massive grazing animals, but what invertebrate feasts there would have been in dung pats weighing eleven kilograms. After the last Ice Age in Western Europe, including in our own country, woodcock would have lived near and benefitted from wild cattle – aurochs – and enjoyed ideal conditions for breeding, with not a single toxic chemical in sight.

The most noticeable thing nowadays is that everything affecting nature has speeded up. Not only are all those large mammals long extinct, but the way we use – or, rather, misuse – the land occurs in such rapid and large-scale ways. There's so little time for these ancient species to adapt to changing times, and with some changes, such as the loss of invertebrates due to toxic chemicals, there is no way they ever can adapt. It's distressing to think that, unless we rapidly change to regenerative agriculture, ban the use of dangerous chemicals and greatly increase ecological restoration, the iconic and familiar woodcock will be lost from most places.

The long life of a knot

The knot is one of the most mobile of species among the waders of the Moray Firth. Big flocks, up to several thousand – in my early years up to 6,000 – return each late summer and spend the winter along our shores. In flight they create the most incredible patterns as they weave and swerve, flashing from white under-parts to pale grey backs. We know the knot as the 'grey knot' but the spring turns them into gorgeous birds, with deep chestnut-red under-parts and a similar colour on the upper parts, spangled with dark brown and grey. It's no wonder Americans call the bird the 'red knot'.

At low tide they search for small marine organisms, often running at the very edge of the incoming tide. This habit lent them their scientific name, *Calidris canutus*, the second word a reference to King Canute, or Cnut the Great, of Denmark, Norway and England (990–1045), who demonstrated to his courtiers that even a king could not prevent the tide from coming in.

This is the story of an outstanding individual bird, its journey across the planet and its remarkably long life.

In the early 1970s I was part of a really great group of birders, who were also bird ringers, in the Scottish Highlands. We formed the Highland Ringing Group and had the opportunity to study the large numbers of wading birds and wildfowl that wintered in the estuaries and on the shores of the Moray Firth. This is a large region, incorporating, from north to south, the Dornoch Firth, the Cromarty Firth, the Beauly Firth and the Inverness Firth, as well as various bays and open shores between Brora and Buckie. We carried out regular counts and even aerial surveys. These were important background studies at a time when there were very active and increasing onshore developments associated with the exploitation of North Sea oil.

The group quickly decided that we should become licensed cannon netters so that we could catch and ring the waders of the area. I had moved with my family to near Munlochy on the Black Isle, which was very handy for these ringing studies on the Moray Firth as well as for my job as Highland Officer with the RSPB.

Our group's biggest ever catch came on 21st October 1978 in the very north of our study area, at Brora in Sutherland. When we arrived, we saw 1,000 knot, 400 bar-tailed godwits and fifteen sanderling, along with other waders on the rocky shore.

We set a net in the best position on the beach while the tide was still a long way out. Cannon netting involves a long wait while the tide comes in and the birds slowly move up onto their high-tide roost. As usual, we kept our fingers crossed that no one would walk along the beach, that no peregrine would come screaming by to flush the whole flock. For once, everything was perfect, the button was pressed, the net flew forward over the flock and we made a very good catch. The team immediately ran down towards the sea and started to extract the birds from the cannon net, while others assembled the hessian keeping cages on the grass above the beach. Our total catch turned out to be 715 knot, thirteen bar-tailed godwits, seven curlew, five redshank, nine dunlin and two turnstone.

Once all the birds were safely in the hessian keeping cages, the team settled down to take biometrics and ring all the birds; it proved to be a long task but it was important that we continued until they had all been released, by which time it was 8pm. We were all exhausted. What we'd done that day, though, set the scene for a fascinating story.

The hundreds of knot that we caught had an interesting age structure, almost seventy-three per cent of them being young birds. The Highland Raptor Group's studies over the years have demonstrated that young birds arrive direct from Greenland to the Moray Firth from late August/early September onwards, whilst the adults migrate to the Wadden Sea in the Netherlands or to the Wash in eastern England to moult, before some of them fly north to the Moray Firth during October. The Moray Firth winter knot population has an above-average percentage of young birds, probably due to many of the adults remaining all winter in the Wadden Sea or on the Wash. We also had four knot in the catch that day which had already been ringed. Three were young birds that had been ringed earlier in the autumn; one at Longman Bay near Inverness, one at Saltburn on the Cromarty Firth and one ringed on 23rd August at Klepp, Rogaland, in south-west Norway. The fourth had been ringed as an adult on the Wash on 22nd August, where it would have been moulting.

In subsequent years, our ringing group re-trapped twenty-five of these birds at a variety of sites around the Moray Firth – Dornoch Point, Nigg Bay, Whiteness Head, Findhorn Bay, Lossiemouth and Buckpool, near Buckie. The oldest of our ringed and locally re-caught knot from the Brora catch was twenty-two years and ninety-nine days, at Buckpool on 28th January 2001.

After our big catch at Brora in 1978, there were twenty-four reports of the ringed birds we caught away from the Moray Firth. These were mostly at moulting or wintering sites: two on the Tay estuary, one on the Firth of Forth, four on the Tees estuary, eight on the Wash, one on the Somme estuary in northern France and five on the Wadden Sea in the Netherlands. We also received reports of three caught and released by bird ringers on spring migration: one in Iceland, one in Germany and one in north Norway.

Occasionally I see summer plumage individuals in Scotland and small returning flocks of failed breeders in July, but an expedition to north-east Greenland in the summer of 1998 gave me the chance to see them on their breeding grounds. We were there on a goose-ringing expedition in late July and into August, when the male parent was the single guardian of the young knot families, the females having migrated earlier. In this Arctic landscape their common wader neighbours were ringed plovers, turnstones, sanderlings and dunlins; all these species also frequent the Moray Firth. When walking on the tundra around Hold with Hope, I often came across a single adult knot poking up from the stones, usually agitated because its young were hidden in the area. I guess I was a lesser threat, though, than wolves, foxes, skuas and ravens, which would predate the young.

The birds I saw in Greenland could have easily been individuals I saw in a flock on the Moray Firth, for we now know that the knot living along the shores of the Moray Firth are from the breeding population of north-east Greenland and eastern Canadian Arctic. The year before our big catch, on 5th September 1977, a foreign ringed knot was found freshly dead at Dornoch Point, just ten miles down the coast from Brora. It had been ringed as a nestling on 17th July that year on the breeding grounds at Zackenberg in north-east Greenland, just a hundred kilometres north of where we later camped at Myggbukta, in the Hold with Hope region.

Zackenberg is 2,000 kilometres north of the Moray Firth. The annual migration flights of knot from the wintering sites to breeding grounds and back is over 5,000 kilometres, and much further if they breed in Canada. One of the young knot that we ringed, CE25745, during that epic catch on 21st October 1978 was seen alive some twenty-seven years, three months and twenty-nine days later in the Netherlands, and set the British Trust for Ornithology's oldest record for this species. The ring was first read by a Dutch birder using a telescope at Den Helder, on 11th February 2005, some 778 kilometres from Brora. It was also identified there on 18th and 19th February 2006.

We do not know how much longer it lived but this was one of the outstanding birds of our catch. That individual in its lifetime would have covered over 130,000 kilometres on its annual migrations, not including its travels around its wintering sites. It would have known many different breeding seasons in Greenland, sunny summers as well as those with late snows. It would have experienced years when the numbers of collared lemming were high – when predators concentrate on lemmings and leave the waders alone – and years of lemming scarcity when male knot have to be very vigilant. I love to think of the summer life of the birds we caught that early autumn day in Brora – the shaggy musk ox for company, the midnight sun, the yapping of Arctic foxes and the howling of polar wolves.

Capercaillies in crisis

The magnificent capercaillie, the largest of the woodland grouse family, lives in conifer forests from Scotland all the way to eastern Siberia. It's nearly as big as a turkey, with the black-plumaged males nearly twice the size of the females. Originally found in Ireland, England and Scotland, it died out in Scotland in the 1800s, probably because it was big and good to eat.

The first reintroduction was in Perthshire in 1837 and the species was restored to much of the country. After the middle of the 20th century there were about 10,000 but by the 1980s, numbers were dropping alarmingly. The increase in non-native conifer planting, forest fences, habitat deterioration, increased predation, wetter weather and human disturbance have all been suggested as reasons for its decline. Now, the capercaillie is in crisis.

The official stated population size is put at around 1,114 birds, with the remaining stronghold in Badenoch and Strathspey, within the Cairngorms National Park. Some of us who have known the species for decades suggest that the true number at the start of the breeding season would be closer to 300 full-grown birds. Additionally, the small, isolated numbers, away from the main centre in Strathspey, should no longer be included in a population estimate as they are no longer viable long-term without major innovative management. There is no doubt that the situation is critical and needs urgent work – now – on the ground. There is no longer time for further research.

In the last thirty years, native pine forest habitat has increased very encouragingly in extent and seedling regeneration, mainly through very effective deer reduction and, in some places, by Scots pine planting schemes. At the same time though, through a lack of grazing, the growth of heather, up to a metre in height, has become extensive and often completely dominates the ground flora. The problem is frequently exacerbated by a thick layer of moss at the base of the heather, covering the earth. Animal tracks have been covered up. In consequence, although adults can survive by feeding in the trees, it is nigh on impossible for female capercaillies to rear broods of young in such inhospitable ground conditions.

The most immediate need is to restore cattle-grazing throughout the pinewoods, in order to replicate the actions of the long-lost native aurochs and the effects of subsequent woodland grazing by crofters' cows that ceased in the latter part of last century. This would restore a whole range of different and essential ecotones within the forest, as well as the animal tracks necessary to allow female capers to lead their young from one good feeding place to the next. Cattle use would also encourage the restoration of blaeberry (and other flowering plants), as it reproduces by rhizomes, quickly colonising bare ground, unlike heather, which seeds. Blaeberry is critical to capercaillies because of the insect life it supports, which feeds the growing poults, while the berries provide essential seasonal food. Some experiments on the use of cattle have been carried out in Glengarry by the Forestry Commission and in Abernethy by the RSPB, but these have been limited in scope. Much greater numbers are required, ranging over much larger areas of the forest.

There needs to be a much greater recognition of the importance of having the pinewoods in good ecological health, and of the fact that this will require some bold actions. In one of the most important breeding areas, Abernethy Forest, relatively small areas have been fenced for seasonal cattle-grazing by commercial stock. To save and restore capercaillies, the whole forest requires cattle-grazing with ring-fencing, with cattle grids on the local roads, as in the New Forest. For ease of management and safety, the cattle should be castrated male Highlanders or similar, untreated with anthelmintics, not fed with supplements and ranging free in herds. They must be outside the requirements of human consumption and allowed to live naturally in their home range throughout their lives. As a start, the whole forest could hold between 300 and 500 free-range cattle in seven to twelve herds, but experience will show whether more or fewer are required. Other key capercaillie forests should be treated in the same way, and the numbers of cattle need to be big, not tentatively small, so that they can create varied and rich habitats for capers and beneficially influence the whole eco-system. The essential large-scale ecosystem benefits will not come about if using short-term commercial cattle treated with chemicals and still destined for human consumption.

The original Caledonian pine forest was not exclusively Scots pine but included a mix – possibly as much as forty per cent – of deciduous trees such as birch, willow, aspen and rowan. Past management and use often selectively favoured Scots pine and removed deciduous trees and shrubs. Although these are regenerating well in many areas, there is a need to increase the amount greatly, by planting and seed dispersal, so as to create an increased availability of deciduous buds, leaves, fruits, nuts and seeds.

One of the dilemmas of capercaillie conservation is the great increase in the use of the bird's habitats by people, because the key capercaillie stronghold in Scotland lies within the Cairngorms National Park. I wrote to the national park authority nearly a decade ago, asking them to agree to refuge areas for breeding capercaillie, but this has not been implemented, despite research showing that human activity in caper forests is markedly damaging. The present nature conservation designations are more likely to encourage people to seek those forests out and use them in preference to non-designated woods, rather than offering capercaillies the protection they need. There is no doubt that the key capercaillie breeding areas should be safeguarded from human disturbance from late March to early September. Dogs should not be allowed in these key areas, even on leads, and intrusive sports activities, such as night-time mountain biking, the use of electric bikes and wild camping, must be excluded from the main capercaillie woods. The numbers of visitors will only increase with the dualling of the A9 truck road and because of the greater likelihood of visits by domestic tourists as a result of the pandemic.

The capercaillie population is now so low and the future for the species looks so perilous that the impact of all predators must be reconsidered and solutions found. It is extremely difficult to manage populations of rare creatures like this when parts of the ecosystem are missing and have been for many long years. Middle-guild predators like fox, badger, pine marten and otter are no longer killed or have their behaviour controlled by the original larger carnivores such as wolf, lynx and brown bear. Following the extinction of the apex predators in Scotland, human persecution severely depleted the middle-guild predators until the middle of the last century, when legal protection started to change their distribution and numbers. With the exception of foxes and crows, they are no longer killed by humans. Within special zones to restore capercaillies it will be necessary to reduce or remove middle-guild predators, while it would also be essential to reintroduce lynx as soon as possible.

With shrinking and often isolated capercaillie populations, there will be increasing problems with the gene pool and possibly with sibling non-breeding behaviour, further exacerbated by an insufficient production of fledged young for dispersal between breeding groups. There is already a clear need to boost the capercaillie population in Scotland with new imports of unrelated birds from Scandinavia, to enhance genetic diversity.

This, though, would probably be of little value if the major changes, as above, were not carried out. Assuming dramatic changes are undertaken, then an import of 500 capercaillie eggs for hatching, or a large import of young birds, would be essential and appropriate.

There's no doubt that the capercaillie is on a knife-edge and could again become extinct. This time, though, it would not be due to ignorance, but because of a lack of determined and enthusiastic management. There is no time now for more research, no time for further dithering, or this iconic bird will once again be lost.

Pears for bears

My earliest childhood memories involve clambering into apple trees to eat the ripe fruit. Climbing into trees that belonged to someone else was so commonplace that it even had its own word, 'scrumping'. It was odd how those ones always tasted nicer.

Fruit orchards were plentiful in Hampshire at that time. We had a largish one in the front garden and another right at the bottom of the smallholding, on the far side of a small stream that ran down into the Solent. Even at that young age, I knew to search for a tree called Beauty of Bath, which was always the earliest apple to ripen, its skin rosy pink. That was as far as my apple knowledge went: there was a gorgeous, much larger and very juicy yellow apple that grew in a really tall tree, but I didn't know its name. All I needed to know was that to get to the fruit meant a long climb, high into the springy branches. I can still recall sinking my teeth into one of the best while perching in the treetop.

Like many other smallholdings in wartime, orchards provided important food for my family and friends, so I've always had an interest in apples, plums, cherries and pears. I'm known for it in the family: when I was watching fruit bats in northern Australia with my daughter and had the joy of picking ripe mangoes from a tree for the very first time, we joked that I must have been a fruit bat in an earlier life.

Here at home in Moray, there was just one plum tree in the garden when we bought this house nine years ago. Since then, I've been planting steadily and now have seven apple trees, eleven plums and two pears. I don't really expect the pears to produce ripe fruit this far north, but they might some day, and we certainly enjoy the apples and plums. The latter can crop so well that there's sometimes a glut, but part-cooked and bottled they bring the sunshine of summer to many a winter meal.

In several places where I monitor osprey nests in late July, I come across gean trees – wild cherries – some laden with beautiful, black, juicy fruit. In the last twenty years or more, this tree has been included in deciduous plantings and now, in some years, they have great crops. I get such pleasure from reaching up to pick a big handful, crushing them in my mouth to get the juice and spitting out the pips, leaving a tell-tale stain on my tongue.

Locally, the most obvious wild harvester of cherries is the pine marten, which leave their distinctive scats, full of cherry stones, along the forest tracks. Fruit trees provide great food for a range of wildlife, either while still on the trees or as fallen fruit. The wild fruit harvest in Britain feeds a variety of creatures, from flocks of starlings hungrily stripping the wild cherries, to badgers, fieldfares, redwings, rodents and slugs, all eating fallen apples in autumn and winter. Long ago, of course, it would have fed brown bears.

This reminds me of some osprey friends in northern Spain, who told me about a fantastic project planting new fruit and chestnut trees in the mountains there. Higher altitude small farms and holdings were being abandoned as the young moved to the towns and villages, with the consequent loss of aged fruit trees. To counteract this loss, one of the progressive conservation groups was planting a succession of fruit and nut trees to the highest levels possible in the mountains, with the aim of providing a successional food supply for the brown bears, as well as bringing other wildlife benefits. I just loved their work and it's very heartening to learn that the brown bear population has increased to over 300 animals.

Over my lifetime it has been sad, when I go south, to see many ancient orchards grubbed up. There are, of course, plenty of commercial orchards in Britain, but the trees are younger and grown to make for easy picking, unlike the old, gnarled trees, so brilliant for wildlife, which I remember from my childhood.

I'm a great believer that we need more fruit trees so that we can eat more locally grown fruit – it's what we should be doing to live more sustainable lives. Local fruit is so much better than some supermarket import from a far-off place. I was shocked when I searched the web for information on my old favourite, Beauty of Bath. They are beautiful eating apples, said the website, but they don't last long. Because they ripen early, they have to compete with late-season apples from the southern hemisphere. Yet transporting fruit over thousands of miles may not be a sensible idea when we have our own fruit trees, especially if we're prepared to eat in season.

On my first visit to East Germany in Communist times, I was struck by the number of fruit trees growing along many of the roads. As I drove, it seemed I passed along never-ending avenues of plum tree, pear tree, apple tree, repeated for miles. I guessed the trees belonged to the local communities and people knew exactly which trees were theirs, for harvesting fresh fruit, bottling for winter and making wine. They were evidence that orchards – in that case, linear ones – are a great standby, especially in difficult times.

Here in Britain, there are encouraging signs that people are planting more fruit and nut trees. Some years ago, I was asked to open a public space and picnic area on the Dava Way, one of the walking routes through Moray. The local volunteers had made a lovely job of it and had planted some trees around the picnic tables. I was disappointed, though, that they had planted birch and rowans, two of our most common deciduous trees. I encouraged them to plant fruit trees along the footpath, both for wildlife and for walkers of the future to reach up and enjoy a fresh apple or plums on their hike. It would be great to do that along all walking routes. Landscaping in our local town, like many new housing areas, includes green space with trees and flowers. The trees are usually ornamental birch and rowans, but how much better it would be if they were fruit and nut trees.

On a much larger scale, it is important to plant far more fruit and nut trees in rewilding schemes, adding so many ecological benefits through their blossoms and fruits. I would encourage the owners and managers of land to be bold and to plant large mixed orchards in wild places among the forests of the future. It's encouraging that people are beginning to collect cuttings from native wild fruit trees, propagating them and planting them to create wild apple, plum and pear groves. As they age, fruit trees become even more wildlife-friendly, providing holes and hiding places for nature. And would it not be marvellous if some of these fruit trees in the future provided food for reintroduced brown bears? And if you need a slogan for your planting projects, how about 'Pears for Bears'? A conversation starter if ever there was one.

Roy Dennis MBE has unparalled expertise as a field naturalist, having worked in conservation, rare species tracking and species reintroductions, as well as directing projects for the RSPB and other organisations. As a broadcaster and educator, he has made documentaries and been a regular presenter on the BBC's *Autumnwatch* and *Springwatch*, as well as other programmes. His Wildlife Foundation of 25 years' standing is internationally recognised for its work in conservation and wildlife reintroductions. Their present reintroduction of the majestic white-tailed eagles to the Isle of Wight, after an absence of 240 years, is ground-breaking and hugely appreciated.

To find out more about the Roy Dennis Wildlife
Foundation, please visit: roydennis.org

Cottongrass Summer, the companion to this
collection of essays, is available from bookshops,
and for UK-based readers, from saraband.net
and the Roy Dennis Wildlife Foundation.